"*Selling Without Sellin₂* work yet. Every Christian business man and woman needs to add this masterpiece to their personal library. It is a jewel! One thing I like about this book that sets it above other Christian business books is that it drives you to the Bible and not away from it. This is a book that I can see me going back to again and again for years. There are many great lessons to live and grow by. A great big thank you to my friend John Grogan."
—*Jim Dale, Professional Speaker, Trainer and Speech Coach*

"What an inspiring and powerful book! This amazing new book by John Grogan is a must-read for both the experienced, as well as the novice, sales professional. John has written a testament to the power of faith in following God's master plan, both in one's professional and personal lives."
—*Jeff Hite, Nashville Convention & Visitors Bureau*

"This book is an excellent resource for anyone working in sales and striving to maintain a Christian witness. John Grogan provides great insight and wisdom into the challenges of the sales profession and our personal lives. It is built on the timeless truth of the Bible and interspersed with John's delightful sense of humor. He inspires and equips Christian sales professionals to be successful and faithful at the same time. I highly recommend it!"
—*M. Katherine Tack, Owner, Advantage Career Resources*

SELLING
WITHOUT
SELLING
YOUR SOUL

JOHN GROGAN

Evergreen
PRESS

Selling Without Selling Your Soul
by John Grogan
Copyright ©2005 John Grogan

ISBN 1-58169-185-8
For Worldwide Distribution
Printed in the U.S.A.

Evergreen Press
P.O. Box 191540 • Mobile, AL 36619
800-367-8203

Table of Contents

Acknowledgments

It is difficult to imagine that any author could have a more dedicated publisher than I have been blessed with. Brian Banashak along with his dear wife and partner, Kathy, have worked tirelessly in getting a great many books to bookstores and other sources in order to empower people for breakthrough living. I am privileged to be counted among the stable of top flight authors under the banner of Evergreen Press.

Special mention is warranted also for Jeff Banashak and his wife Rosa who work diligently behind the scenes to insure that Evergreen Press fulfils its mission to provide education for personal growth.

Dedication

This book is dedicated to those who put integrity over expediency, people before profit, and character above cleverness; that special breed who don't do it their way, but do their work as unto the Lord. These people not only know what it's like to be riding high in April and shot down in May, but struggle day to day with faithfulness and consistency as they strive to compete with competitors who seem to have discarded their moral compasses.

If life isn't for sissies, it is doubly true for those in sales. As anyone who's been on the playing field any length of time has discovered, we salespeople experience higher highs and lower lows than most of those around us. We enter the arena every day to face one of the most savage adversaries in life: rejection. Wisdom born of experience has taught us that sales is the lowest paying easy work and the highest paying hard work there is.

ARE YOU A SALESPERSON?
Someone has said that salespeople can be a big problem to their bosses, their mates, conservative credit managers, hotels, and sometimes to each other. They live in hotels and motels, on airplanes, in buses, cars and cabs. They are reported to sleep before, during, and after business hours. In many ways they are a tribute to themselves.

They come at the most inopportune times under the slightest pretext, stay longer under more opposition, ask more personal questions, make more comments, put up with more inconveniences, and take more for granted under greater resistance than any other group or body, including the united states army.

They make more noise and mistakes, correct more errors, adjust more differences, explain more discrepancies, bear more grievances, pacify more belligerents and lose more time under high pressure (without losing their own tempers) than any class we know, including ministers.

They introduce more new goods, dispose of more old goods, load more freight cars, unload more ships, build more factories, start more new businesses and write more debits and credits in our ledgers than any other group in America.

And when buyers or customers, sellers or clients, find themselves in a tight spot, they usually pick out from among their salesman friends, one of several in whom they have complete confidence and trust for their counsel and advice, and they get it clean and straight. Are you a salesman?

Introduction

In all my years of sharing sales techniques, whether in a seminar setting or a convention breakout session, sales people have asked me this question: How do I survive out there with the sharks? How do I compete in a "win-at-any-cost, look out for number one" world? Let me assure you, you don't have to make a Faustian deal with the devil to excel. There is a way to do it right. We can have life and have it more abundantly.

While we cannot play softball on a hardball field, we must ask ourselves, "Whom do I trust?" Whose report will I believe? *Selling Without Selling Your Soul* is a resource book that will show you how to sell without surrendering your soul. It will show you great techniques to use and not manipulate or take advantage of your customers and clients.

If we cannot obey the laws that are written on the tablets of our minds and hearts, there is little hope for us.

More than a teacher I see myself as an awakener. Most of us need reminding more than things new. You will find on these pages "how-to-do's"rather than "what-to-do's."

—*John Grogan, 2005*

Chapter One

Set Your Sail With Goals

Choices, not chance, determine our destiny. Whether we're selling a product or a service, we offer the customers either one or more choices in the marketplace. The selling profession centers around convincing others that the choices we represent are the best ones for them.

But what about the choices that we ourselves make? One of the most important decisions we will ever make in life is the choice of whose voice we will listen to. Whose shouts or whispers will govern our steps? There are four choices and the one we select will determine how life turns out for us because the voice we listen to will influence our priorities.

The first voice that clamors to be heard is our own. This

1

is the voice in our head that endlessly cries out — I want it! I need it!

The second voice is the voice of the world. Spend, spend, it shouts — you deserve it...you're worth it! Buy to gratify. More is better! Bigger is better! Newer is better!

The third voice is the one that appeals to our lower nature, always enticing us to let our appetites rule over us. This one attempts to sell us on the idea of compromising our Christian values. Its objective is to push God to the margins and fill the center of our page with cravings for money, sex, and power.

The fourth voice is the quiet still voice of the Holy Spirit. Always the gentleman, He never attempts to out-shout the other voices. A quiet and contemplative time is a good setting in which to hear this voice. But we can hear Him anywhere, even in the midst of a hectic day with the cell phone constantly jangling its tune at us. Sometimes we just need to take a minute and calm our thoughts and compulsions in order to listen. Many people take time early in the morning before they get into the traffic of their day to spend time alone with God. It has been my experience that God speaks more in persistent whispers than in perceptible shouts.

Builder or Bandit?

Which voice we choose to listen to will determine whether we're a builder or a bandit. The builder dreams of all they can do. The bandit dreams of all the things they can get. One's a giver; one's a taker. In the profession of selling, this translates into either loving people (in the sense of respecting and serving them) and using money, or loving money and using people.

At one point when I perceived that I was at the height of my career, I had all the appearances of success, but suffered the barrenness of emotional and spiritual depravation. When I arrived at what I thought was the top of the mountain, I was extremely fatigued. Due to my own poor choices, everything came crashing down around me. I was forced by my desperate circumstances to rethink my priorities.

Two conclusions emerged. The first one is that many people see little need to include God in their lives when they're making good speed through calm seas. God is easy to ignore when our sails are full of wind and our most pressing decisions involve things like what luxury nameplate to drive this year, or what exotic spa to travel to next holiday season.

The second realization was that when we see the masses heading in the same direction, we can almost be sure that we should be heading in the opposite one. There is a truth about communal madness. Mere numbers can never determine what is right and true. The masses are too many times heading in the wrong direction.

Our Priorities

Whether core values shape our priorities or our priorities influence our core values, one thing is true: God universally rejects the idea that the end justifies the means. Justifying the means to gain our objective is debased morality. It's weak tea that satisfies no one in the end. On the other hand, I have found that if we order our values correctly by listening to the right voice, our character will change. This change leads to wholeness, which promotes enduring satisfaction.

Who our god is will influence our priorities. Money, sex, sports, power — whatever dominates our thoughts and our speech will dictate who or what stands center stage in our life. If we live sports, we talk sports. If we live politics, we talk politics. If we live for money, that's all we think about, talk about...and worry about. When we speak, not only are our minds on parade, but what's in our hearts as well. The trip from the head to the heart is, on average, 16 inches. The trip from the heart to the mouth is about 12 inches. Luke 6:45 tells us that out of the overflow of a man's heart his mouth speaks. We cannot hide for long what is in our hearts.

So, before we formulate plans to attain our goals, we must first clarify if life for us means more than the acquisition and ownership of things. There is no doubt that God wants us to have prosperity in our lives, but that means balance, because any strength taken to an extreme becomes a liability or a weakness.

A Hebrew proverb says that we come into life with clinched fists and go out with open hands. God's Word says that if we first seek Him and His righteousness — right priorities — our needs will be met. It strikes me that before we go surfing off in quest of great expectations, perhaps we should give some thought to God's priorities. It's not only arrogant but also dangerous to push our blueprints under the Potter's nose, looking for his imprimatur on our plans.

Our Perspective Frames Our Goals

Listening to the right voice and establishing right priorities will result in a right perspective. And a right perspective will insure that God will direct our steps in framing our goals.

Priorities have a great bearing on our plans and the formation of our goals. Goals move us beyond the present; they get us out of a maintenance mode and enable us to actively pursue our mission. Our mission of accomplishing worthwhile objectives is realized by our industry, diligence, and productivity.

5

I once had a salesperson on my staff who had only two things going for him, but they proved to be quite enough. He had an indomitable spirit and a strong commitment to goals. He would put his warm feet out on the cold floor, saying, "Good morning, God!" rather than, "Good God, it's morning!" Many times he'd cut himself shaving because he was in such a hurry to get to the office. Now many of us would call someone like that a fanatic! But in one sense, a fanatic can just be someone who's more committed to something than we are.

He instinctively knew that without goals to get him to a specific pre-determined destination, he would operate with good intentions but flounder because he would lack direction. This is like being lost while driving and thinking that the answer to our dilemma is to speed up. By speeding up we don't find our way, we merely become more lost as we continue in the wrong direction. Blind activity results in empty hope. We can mistake activity for achievement, exchanging the mere appearances of success for worthwhile accomplishments. The devastating result is we are bobbing around on a sea of activity with no destination in mind at all. As soon as any storm threatens our voyage, we get tossed around by the waves and begin to panic when we find that we have no anchor to steady us.

The insidious thing about living without goals is that we quickly become accustomed to it. Like a broken light globe in the bathroom, a missing dresser drawer knob, or the chipped counter top in the kitchen, we lose sight of how things should be. I meet people everyday, and you probably do also, who have become comfortable with being relationally, intellectually, financially and most detrimentally, spiritually poor.

Preparation

An army does not wait until it reaches the front lines of battle before preparing its ordinance, if it did it would quickly be destroyed. Like an army we must prepare ourselves to be ready when we meet opportunity. If we are to achieve our destiny, we have to think seriously about goals because they will carry us to our destiny.

There are four questions we must ask ourselves when forming goals. The first question is WHAT? What is it that I truly am after? To answer this we need knowledge. We need to be forthright in our assessment of our skills, abilities, and giftedness. Ask God to give you knowledge. He says that you have not because you ask not. Then when you ask, He says you ask for the wrong reasons. We want what we want for our glory and not His. For example, if I'm forty-five years old, nearsighted, and have a tendency to get very nervous when things get tense, I probably want to rethink my ambition about becoming a Grand Prix race car driver.

The second question we must ask ourselves is HOW? Exactly how am I going to go about achieving my objective? Planning develops understanding, which helps define the answer to this question. If I feel my talents and interests point me towards dentistry, I might not want to enroll at Massachusetts Institute of Technology.

The third question we have to answer is WHEN? When will I put into play the next logical action step? To answer this question demands prioritizing, which develops our timing. If there is premature execution of part of your plan, things don't gel. If you wait too long, the fruit may have gotten overripe and fallen from the tree.

The fourth question is WHY? For what purpose am I pursuing this? This question, if asked with an honest heart, develops wisdom. Wisdom is being able to understand things from God's perspective. Anything less is blind ambition. Is the trophy worth the chase? Will the trophy stand the test of fire? If it does, it will turn out to be a beautiful crown that we may place at the feet of Christ one day.

Commitment to Our Goals

Setting well-defined goals motivates commitment. Without commitment we lack identity. No identity, no worthwhile productivity. No productivity, no sense of significance. The thing that subverts commitment to anything today is the multiple choices we all have put before us. Because life is so complex and we face so many variables, it's easy to become mercurial; if it doesn't work out quickly or to our immediate gratification, we tend to opt out. This has devastating consequences on marriages, careers, and even our relationship with God. We pray and if we don't have an answer in two weeks we quit, or worse, we go back to our old way of doing things. We leave when we decide to leave. Covenant says that you don't cut and run. Many people today resemble a wandering undisciplined river taking the line of least resistance. This makes for crooked rivers and crooked lives.

If we lack goals in the multiple spheres of our life, i.e. our vocational life, family life, finances, and most importantly, our spiritual life, we forfeit accountability. To the degree we reject accountability, we abandon awareness and become dull, and sluggish. It's as if we sleepwalk through our days. In truth, we squander away our destiny. Goals help us to keep our destination in sharp focus.

This reminds me of a question my wife asked me not long ago. She asked if I ever thought of dying or death. I replied that I think about it every day. She was somewhat startled at my answer. I assured her that I didn't think about it in a morbid way or even a fearful way, but with the realization that life is like a passing shadow; no matter how long we live, life is very brief. If all we have are goals limited to earthly accomplishments, we might fail to achieve eternal triumphs. It is wise to be mindful of our mortality, as it is wise to be good, and good to be wise.

Putting Goals on Paper

I have found it helpful to write out my goals. There's something about writing out our goals that forces us to think in specific, concrete terms rather than in general, abstract terms. Henry Ford said that to think, really think, is one of the hardest things we can do.

Without clarity and resolve to the questions of WHAT, HOW, WHEN, and WHY, we will end up derelicts washed up on the beach, failing to make over the open seas of opportunity to our destination.

This, of course, is not what our God intended. God wants us to be overcomers — to reign and rule — to take dominion and bring order to chaos. Because I, like so many others, wanted to, "Do it my way," as Frank Sinatra's signature song exalts, I learned wisdom through difficult pain. We cannot trust in the things we build with our own hands and for our own security. God calls this idolatry. Employing our abilities is futile without His presence and His goals in our lives. In John 15:5 we read, "I am the vine you are the branch; he who abides in Me, and I in him, will bear much fruit; for apart from Me you can do nothing." God is the great architect and keeper of the blueprints. If He is first in our life He will change our hearts, renew our minds, adjust our attitudes, and influence our desires. This enables us to operate in His strength, under the shelter of His wings (Psalms 91:4).

Chapter Two

Make Time a Useful Resource

Nothing Worthwhile
Ever Came out of Chaos

To a great extent the problem with efficiently handling our time isn't the number of demands on our time, or a lack of skill in scheduling our many appointments, but our values. What is really important?

One of my favorite stories is about a young salesman talking with the owner of a country store. The two men were sitting on the front porch passing the time when suddenly the phone rang. The old storeowner made no attempt to answer it. Thinking the storeowner probably couldn't hear very well, the young salesman gently let him know that his phone was ringing. The old man looked at the salesman and said, "I heard it. I had that thing installed for *my* convenience!"

The modern computer was highly touted as a time and energy saver when it was first introduced, and to be sure, in many ways it is. But what it has really done is enhance our ability to get more work out, thus increasing our workloads and demanding more and more hours. We need to ask ourselves if some of these modern conveniences are our servants or masters.

As innovations in communication technology grow exponentially, I can't help but think that being continuously rushed is a social sickness of our time. The Germans have a saying—An hour in America is 40 minutes in Germany. I see men and women racing to work on the motorways of my city, cell phones planted in their ears, scheduling appointments or wrapping up details to important business I assume. The more skillful can manage this while tooling along at a cool 80 miles an hour.

Perhaps hurrying is a ploy used by the enemy of our souls. Caught up in the tension of traveling at high speed all the time, we resemble the frog in Malcolm Muggeridge's experiment. The frog, failing to perceive the rising temperature of the water, was eventually boiled to death. Like the frog getting comfortable with warmer and warmer temperatures, we get accustomed to activity overload, unsuspecting of the emotional avalanche that it will eventually bring. Physical exhaustion pushes us into emotional exhaustion and we have to bow out of the game. In the world of frogs it's called being cooked. In the world of humans, it's called burnout.

As we mentioned in the last chapter, any strength taken to an extreme becomes a liability or a weakness. There needs to be balance in our lives. We have to wisely orchestrate the parity between our spiritual life, our family life, and our work. These three major spheres are overlapping rings. If one of the spheres is out of round it will adversely affect the other two spheres. It's a little like conducting a three-ring circus.

Here are some practical points to ponder concerning the pursuit of profitability, while at the same time saving your sanity. Consider this, every night at midnight exactly 1,440 minutes are deposited in our time bank. It doesn't matter what our status is, how rich or poor we are, or what our I.Q. is. Time is the great leveler because the same amount is granted to kings, paupers, the wise and the foolish...each midnight we all get 1,440 minutes. What we don't spend wisely by the following midnight, we forfeit. The snag comes in knowing that at midnight we'll receive another time deposit. So we tarry, failing to realize that time is of the essence. God doesn't call us to be rich or successful, as the world would define it. He calls us to be faithful in the use of our time and talents. Life is fleeting, but in the brevity of life we can elect to be faithful.

To make the most of our time we needn't run, run, run! Even a cheetah doesn't run flat out for long. We need to have a plan of action, but it needs to be action with fore-thought. Action for action's sake is the sister of folly.

Ready, Fire Aim!

Here's the real deal: Ready, fire, aim! Surprised? The ready part we have discussed. We need to prepare our-selves with a plan. But fire next? I believe we need to get into action as quickly as possible when the cost to change the outcome is low. Our plan does not have to be perfect, because we can correct our course as we move ahead.

I've had salespeople who were always getting ready to commence to begin to get started perhaps maybe to-morrow. They would make Hamlet look impetuous. They never got beyond making their "perfect plan" and so they were never sure exactly what they should do. They never got their gun out of the holster because they were intent on gauging the wind speed and direction that could affect the bullet's trajectory. I would rather have a salesperson firing in some direction than one standing there with a wind gauge in their hand. I can correct the aim of their gun, but I can't do anything with one that remains in the holster.

We don't drift to achievement but we most assuredly can

drift into a Rip Van Winkle-like hibernation. The parable of the talents is a sobering reminder that we are to be doers and not hearers only (Luke 19:11-26).

Getting into action also helps us avoid another self-delusionary exercise. It's called the scenario game. This is a form of pre-game armchair quarterbacking. We sip that third cup of coffee and speculate: If I do this, this might happen, but if I do that, that might happen, forever planning, never doing. In the gospel of Mark the word "immediately" is used 42 times. This suggests that we should put off procrastination.

When the cost to change the outcome is high we want to take the ready, aim, fire approach. In Luke 14:28 Jesus asks, "For which of you intending to build a tower, does not sit down first and count the cost whether he has enough to finish it." We surely don't want to build a new manufacturing plant only to realize upon completion that we should have built in the south, and with a railroad siding nearby. We can't just pick the thing up and set it down in the right location. But we do tend to over study situations. This malaise is compounded when groups are involved. Committees, the old comedian Fred Allen said, are made up of people who individually can do nothing, and together decide that nothing can be done. Perhaps that's a bit overstated, but my experience confirms that the larger the group, the more it's like herding cats to get a consensus.

On the other hand, we can't just be action junkies or people who continuously thrive on activity. I call them firefighters. These are people who love to fight the daily fires of business, and if there are no fires to fight, they'll start one so they'll have something to do. They go home at the end of the day feeling spent but fulfilled. Unfortunately fulfilled and fruitful are not one and the same. They are little closer to meaningful accomplishments at the end of the day than when they awoke that morning.

Perfectionism Can Waste Time

In addition to activity with significance to the plan, we need to major in the majors by striving for *effectiveness* rather than perfection. An inveterate perfectionist will drive others crazy. I had a business associate once who would actually straighten pictures on clients' walls. He would of course ask the client's permission, but this was done as he made his way to his self-appointed mission. Once while having lunch with this associate, he bolted from his chair as a patron walked by on his way to pay his bill. The man was totally unaware that he had his dinner napkin still tucked into his belt. Not to worry, my friend, gallant defender of the uninformed, raced to save this man from further social embarrassment. The man, thinking he was being assailed, jumped back, hitting a woman's elbow and sending a full cup of coffee flying all over the front of her husband's resplendent suit. In the resulting chaos I quietly slipped out a side entrance. Perfectionism is one of the most patent examples of majoring in the minors. We do not have a mandate to pick lint off other people or wipe their noses.

A lesser degree of perfectionism is excessive efficiency. People who are overly precise tend to focus on the best way to do a job. A person majoring in the majors focuses on the best job to do. The effectiveness expert knows that roughly 80 percent of their results come from 20 percent of the things they do. The well-intentioned are preoccupied with many trivial matters. The successful concentrate on a few vital matters.

Schedules Create Productive Atmospheres

Another characteristic of the achiever is to be pleasant with people but brutal about time. Most highly effective people reserve the right to maintain their schedules. Productive people don't let other peoples urgencies become their urgencies. (I'm not talking about important interruptions or urgent matters but things that can wait.) Socializing is important in building the social fabric, but we should do it at our convenience and not at the convenience of others. Time is a commodity that God expects us to steward.

Many managers keep what they call an *open door policy*, which implies that anyone has free access to them at any time. With continual interruptions they're always just getting started.When I had a sales staff I had what came to be known as a *screen door policy*. Not wanting to hide behind closed doors or sit with my back continually to my door, I created certain time zones when my people could wander in and have my undivided attention.

Think of time in terms of segments, say 15 minutes to a segment. Minutes fly by too quickly to monitor, but 15-minute chunks of time are manageable. How many segments of time, for example, will I take to rehash yesterday's sports with people in the office who are never going to buy anything from me? Or how many segments will I take for lunch today?

Keep a daily planner. Don't try to commit seldom needed information like your license plate number to memory. The great Albert Einstein was once mildly chided for having to look up his own telephone number in the directory. His response was that since there were so many reference sources — in the form of phone books — he didn't wish to use valuable memory space for such things. There are people who can recite baseball statistics from 1968 or tell you who won the Stanley Cup in hockey every year since the custom was first established. When we need this information we can call the library.

We should hide a memorized Scripture verse or verses in our heart to sustain us in a time of our need. Romans 15:13 is excellent: "May You fill me with all joy and peace as I place my trust in you Father. Then I will overflow with hope by the power of the Holy Spirit."

If it is our hearts' desire to walk pleasing before the Lord — the giver and sustainer of life — then one of the time thieves we will have to deal with is the telephone. If you are like many salespeople, you have no doubt discovered that it is very difficult to talk to live people today. This, in part, is due to cutbacks in personnel. One person is now often doing the work of three people. In many smaller to mid-size companies the receptionist not only is responsible for incoming calls but has multiple other tasks as well. In some cases incoming calls bypass the receptionist — who, in most cases, is busier than a short tail cow during fly season, and goes directly into voice mail. This can be maddening for people calling in, but this is the tenor of our times.

But what about outgoing calls? For purposes of returning phone calls we need to think in terms of three categories: 1) Those receiving a good shot; 2) Those receiving a better shot; 3) Those who should receive our best shot. The people entitled to a good shot receive a return call at our convenience. The people qualifying for a better shot receive a return call today. Those entitled to our best shot receive a call as soon as we can break away from what preoccupies us. This last category always should include customers and clients. I make it an incontestable policy to always take a call from my wife and children regardless of whom I'm with because they know not to impose on my work time with a frivolous call.

Time — we can't save it or parlay it; all we can do is spend it. Yesterday is a cancelled check; tomorrow is a promissory note; only today is legal tender. Martin Luther said, "There are two days — today and that day." We need to think, plan, and execute wisely for one day we will have to give an accounting.

Chapter Three

Principles of the Universe

Nature Tolerates No Long-term Robberies

When I was a little tyke I wondered if I could stand on a giant boulder as it fell through space and step off just before it hit the earth without getting hurt. I was ignorant. If I were still puzzling over this today I might be considered stupid.

A number of years ago a truck was making its way down a dusty road in the deepest part of Africa. Riding in the back of the truck were several men who had never ridden in a vehicle before. When the truck approached the place where the men were to get off, they stepped off the back of the truck. Several were injured because they did not understand the laws of physics. Were these men stupid? No, they were simply ignorant about the law of gravity.

We would be flabbergasted if any person in our society lacked this kind of understanding. Yet, many people today fail to use eternal principles of success that have been around since God created the universe and all that is in it. These principles apply equally to everyone at all times everywhere. Like the laws of physics they are unalterable and to ignore them is like playing Russian roulette with only one empty chamber.

Principles of the universe are standards of established order. These are laws put into place by God to bring order out of chaos. There are laws of logic, laws of chemistry, laws of nature, social laws, mathematical laws, moral laws, and spiritual laws. We refer to these as principles or guidelines because we have a tendency to view laws as restrictive and negative. I think it would be a fair assessment to say that most people today, especially here in the land of the free and the brave, bristle over the word "law."

Nevertheless, working in harmony with some of these laws will dramatically improve our chances for abundance. It's interesting that there are people who are oblivious to these laws but are using them to their great prosperity. Others, who are aware of these laws and are failing to use them, struggle throughout life.

Law of Inertia

The first law that we want to look at is the Law of Inertia. This law states that a body at rest tends to stay at rest unless acted upon by an outside force. Some people have the motivation of desperation, caused by spending their commissions before they have it in their hands.

While doing a seminar in England a number of years ago I noticed a memo posted on the bulletin board. It read: The company regrets to announce that it has come to our attention that sales people are dying on the job and failing to fall down. This practice must stop as it becomes impossible to distinguish between death and normal movement of the staff. In the future any salesperson found dead in an upright position will be dismissed from the company.

When I was a young salesman I struggled with this Law of Inertia. Some invisible force seemed to be holding me back. Finally, I realized that it was a lack of faith. Limited faith is based on circumstances and the fear of failure. Fear of failure keeps our successes at a distance. Then two things happened that changed my fortunes. The greatest was letting God do business with me. This happened in 1980. I had been a Christian since I was a small boy, but somehow I only knew about God, and until that day I didn't have a personal day-to-day walking relationship with Him.

The second epiphany I had was of a business nature. Someone introduced me to the "Rule of Six." This rule states that a prospect has to experience six contacts, on the average, before they take an action. Most sales people simply don't persist long enough. They try one, two, maybe three times, and then give up.

The Law of Motion

Persistence introduced me to a second principle of success: the Law of Motion. This law states that a body in motion tends to stay in motion. We know it as momentum. A locomotive will expend a 100% energy output in overcoming inertia. Once it's rolling down the rails, it only requires a 9% energy output to keep moving. The idea is to avoid coming to a full stop to conserve energy. Continually starting up is immensely stressful and costly. Keep the momentum going, even if it's only "falling forward" momentum. The smallest step is better than the noblest intention. Start where you are, do what you can, and God will meet you there. Charles Spurgeon, the great English Baptist preacher said that by persistence the snail reached the ark. It isn't how fast we come out of the blocks in the race of life; it's if we continue to run the race.

What is fast anyway? The snail riding atop the turtle is apt to be breathless with the speed of his journey. And if it isn't what we get out of life but what we become, why are we in such a hurry to get through it? *Festina Lente* is Latin for, "Make haste slowly."

If we make our plans but God directs our steps, why do we scheme and sweat so much? It excites my curiosity as to whether God is amused over some of our puny minded efforts. I am persuaded however that if we do not involve Him in our plans, it does make Him sad.

Another thing we have to recognize in running this marathon of life, God doesn't fault us for falling down, but it bothers Him when we remain down or wallow in self-pity and defeatism. One of my favorite verses in scripture is Proverbs 24:10: "If you falter in times of trouble, how small is your strength!" God wants us to try. "Though I fall, I will rise again," Micah tells us in chapter seven verse eight. "When I sit in darkness, the Lord himself will be my light."

Distractions are the enemy of our persistence. We take our eyes off the prize. Any number of things can sabotage our focus. When we were kids we would hold a magnifying glass over a piece of paper, collecting the sun's energy to focus on a single spot. It wasn't long before a hole would appear, then widen into flame. I have seen many salespeople fall short of success because they failed to keep their focus on a single objective long enough to burn through to success.

The Bible speaks of this in a curious way. In Matthew 11:12 it says: "the kingdom of heaven suffers violence, and the violent take it by force." The exact meaning of this verse, according to theologians, is open to speculation. One interpretation suggests that it refers to persistence; that men lay hold of the kingdom, not unlike Jacob who wrestled with a man until daybreak. And when the man saw that he had not prevailed against him, said, "Let me go, for the dawn is breaking." But Jacob said, "I will not let you go unless you bless me." So the man said to him, "What is your name?" And he said, "Jacob" (which means deceiver or Grabber). And the man said, "Your name shall no longer be Jacob, but Israel (one who prevails with God), for you have striven with God and with men and have prevailed."

Persistence empowers us to endure. The word endurance is taken from two Greek words — "up" and "hold," or to uphold. This is a military term conveying the idea of bearing up under trying circumstances and not fainting, collapsing, or suffering the loss of courage, or to carry on without forsaking hope and succumbing to fear and doubt.

I remember asking my brother Thomas shortly after rededicating my life to Jesus Christ, when could I expect to get off the emotional roller coaster of life — sky-high one day, reaching up to touch bottom the next. He told me that God doesn't want us getting off the roller coaster. He wants us to hang on and He will level off the hills, fill in the valleys, and make our roadway straight. God could do this in an eye blink, but then we would never learn to soldier (see Jeremiah 12:5).

Law of Use

A third principle of the universe is the Law of Use. Just as the muscles in a broken limb will atrophy because of non-use, a talent or gift will become not as useful if we ignore them. While we don't forget how to type, ride a bicycle, swim, or play the violin, lack of use over an extended period of time dulls our proficiency, and the value of our talent, gift, or skill fades.

Practice! Practice! Practice! Once after a concert a woman came up to the Russian pianist, Vladimir Horowitz, and gushed how she would love to be able to play the piano like him. "No, you wouldn't" the great artist answered. Somewhat taken aback, the woman persisted that she would. "No," Horowitz replied, "You wouldn't be willing to practice every day for eight hours." While some people possess greater inherent abilities than others, there is no such thing as a natural born salesperson, anymore than there are natural born doctors or space scientists. Highly skilled salespeople are made not born. You will never read in the birth announcements of your local newspaper where someone gave birth to a healthy, eight pound, bouncing baby salesman.

Highly skilled salespeople practice and hone their skills much like any artist. A speaker friend of mine, Jim Dale, told me about his "Get Good Room." He has a special room in his home where he goes and practices his craft. He is always busy because he's a pro.

Law of Reciprocity

A fourth law that is indispensable is the Law of Reciprocity. Sometimes referred to as the Law of Mutual Exchange, this law states that anyone who helps another to prosper must themselves prosper. The Bible expresses it this way in Luke 6:38: "If you give, you will get! Your gift will return to you in full and overflowing measure, pressed down, shaken together to make room for more, and running over. Whatever measure you use to give — large or small — will be used to measure what is given back to you" (*Life Application Bible*).

If you pour out your cup, God will give you a bigger cup. What is in the cup? Compassion, courtesy, forgiveness, mercy, money, kindness, service, giving. The best definition of friendship is giving time to someone. If we extend the kindness of time and knowledge, our customers and clients will reciprocate by entrusting us with their business.

If people get a sense that you really care, they will throw money in your backyard just to see what you'll do with

it. Caring and love are decisions, not some mawkish sen-
timentality. The head cannot fake what the heart does
not feel. People can tell if we are disingenuous.

Law of Diminishing Returns

There is one more law that we must reckon with. This is
the Law of Diminishing Returns. The essence of this law
says that a need fulfilled is no longer a motivating force.
This law can spur us onto bigger and better successes or
act as a tripwire. If this law were not at work, babies
would have no interest in learning how to walk. Students
would never desire to move on to the next level, much
less graduate. The Columbus of space exploration would
not be curious about what lies beyond the moon.
Salespeople would never strive for excellence. Everyone
would be satisfied exactly where he or she is. But the
law of diminishing returns drives us on. It is human nature to want to expand our horizons.

This very same law, however, can work against us when
it concerns our appetites. In the world of selling we can
very easily move from a sense of service to one of greed.
Because of a lack of vigilance, we can shift from serving
people to using them. While doing research for this
book, I worked for a large, national automobile dealership. We, the salespeople, would always ask each other
how many cars we sold. We could easily start keeping
score: how many cars, how many units, how much

volume, how much money did everyone make? If we lose sight of filling needs, we can look forward to small time gains rather than big time rewards. There is no right way to do a wrong thing.

Appearance attracts, money attracts, and power attracts. An old adage, originally intended for pastors, is wise counsel for us all, in view of the times in which we live: Beware of the three G's: The gold, the glory, and the girls (or guys). All three can lead us away into captivity.

Regarding social interaction with receptionists, secretaries, or handsome delivery drivers, flirtation can lead to advanced come-ons or suggestive overtures. These kinds of things have no place in the Christian's life. Can a person take hot coals to their chest and not be burned? It is our responsibility to be ambassadors for the living God. Some people are in the house and some are outside the house. If they are in the house we have to be extraordinarily careful that we do not cause them to stumble or fall (see Mark 9:42).

Solomon tells us in Proverbs 4:23, "above all else, guard your affections, for they influence everything else in your life. Spurn the flattering lips of a loose woman." We could add, spurn also the spurious advances of a profligate male. Watch your step. Stick to the path and be safe. Don't get sidetracked; pull back your foot from danger. The time to resolve the matter is long before the encounter. Once you're in deep mud it is too late, for when temptation strikes and desire is aroused, we don't want counsel, we want satisfaction.

For those outside the house of God, it should arouse a deep sense of compassion within us, for they are missing the whole purpose of life. Are we to be exploiters, manipulating and using for our own vanities, or are we distressed over the numbers in the street stumbling towards the slaughter? God does not give us comfort in order to make us comfortable; He gives us comfort in order to bring comfort to others. Moreover, he does not enable us to see with the eyes of our hearts in order to judge or hold others in contempt. Compassion and kindness, the Talmud tells us, is the highest wisdom.

God has set these laws in motion and just as we need oil to help an engine run smoothly, we need to follow the inherent commands of His laws so that our lives can be blessed by Him.

Chapter Four

Generate Loyalty

Do we want to survive with the sharks or excel with the saints?

There were two drugstores located a block away on either side of an elementary school. When kids bought candy from the one store, the merchant would dip his scoop into the large candy case, empty it onto the scales, and then begin removing candy until the exact amount ordered was indicated on the scales. The other storeowner purposefully kept from putting enough candy on the scales. He would keep adding more and more candy until the right amount ordered was reached. To his young customers it looked like they were getting more candy at the second store. The first store eventually went out of business. The second store was always full of kids.

Look for ways to give added value to your customers and clients. Like the kids in the candy store, added value can sometimes be a matter of perception rather than a fact. One way to give added value is to discover what your competition is doing and — in most cases — simply do the opposite. Think creatively about how to give greater service.

Sometimes when I'm speaking to a group I will have them do this little exercise:

O O O
O O O
O O O

The objective is to use four perfectly straight lines and pass through the exact center of each circle. You are not allowed to lift your pen or pencil from the paper, erase, or retrace. You will find the answer at the back of this book, but first see if you can solve it. This little exercise will cause you to think creatively if you want to solve it correctly.

There's a story about a small merchant squeezed between two large competitors. One day this merchant noticed that the storeowner on his left has put up a large banner on the front of his building reading: FIRE SALE! A few days later, the merchant on his right puts up an equally large banner saying: GOING OUT OF BUSINESS SALE! The little storeowner is beside himself trying to think of how he could compete with the big boys. After a great deal of pacing, a jolt of brilliance overcame his confusion. He put up a sign over his front door: MAIN ENTRANCE! The masses do not think outside the box. Think outside the box. Live on the edge; color outside the lines.

Winning Big With Customers

Two examples of thinking outside the box will put you leagues ahead of your competition: *Promise long and deliver short,* or said another way, under promise and over deliver. Most people have this backwards. They tell the customer or client the goods will be delivered on Tuesday, but it arrives on Monday of the following week, if that early!

The second way to win big with your prospects, customers, and clients, is to love people and use money and things. As we mentioned in the last chapter, many companies and the sales representatives who work for them, have this exactly reversed. Love is a choice of the will, not a feeling. Feelings follow action. First a resolve, then an action, and then the feeling. Love is the greatest of all human qualities. It involves unselfish service to others; love's greatest message gives evidence that we truly care. Love always precedes joy, peace, patience, kindness, goodness, gentleness, faithfulness, and self-control. Love never fails.

The reason love never fails is that love is a verb; love acts, love fosters concern and concern serves, perhaps, without even having to be asked. If I say that I love my wife, yet never run the sweeper, empty the dishwasher, mop the kitchen floor (which hurts her back), or clean a commode, I have a noun love, not a verb love. Love isn't love until you give it away.

Four Levels of Service

Love will drive us into service. There are four levels of service:

1) HIDE and SEEK. People who have a job rather than a mission or a calling are gathered into this category. They perform their assigned tasks in a perfunctory way. Unfortunately, the masses park here. But this is good news for someone like you because the field of competition is not crowded.

2) The second level of service is called SURRENDER. This is when we have that clerk cornered and by our mere persistence, force them to break away from their conversational partner and wait on us.

3) The third level of service is VOLUNTARY. This is where the clerk, waiter, or other service provider, approaches voluntarily with perhaps a pleasant smile and evidences genuine interest in helping us.

4) The highest level of service possible is ASSUMPTIVE service. To reach this level we have to know a person's needs in advance. An example of this is the administrative assistant or secretary who makes flight arrangements for his or her boss before being asked to do so. These people are worth their weight in titanium.

Kindness and Loyalty

In addition to providing a good level of service, two other qualities will result in loyalty among customers and clients: good will and trust. Good will, unlike value, which pertains to tangible assets, is intangible. It is a salable asset arising from the reputation of a business or individual and the relationship they have with their customers. If the public's perception of a company is poor, the chances of that companies representative overcoming this bias is remote.

I have a friend who resigned her position with an industry giant in the technology field because she couldn't offer effective tech support once she made the sale. She knows you cannot separate character from conduct — that a company or individual will act out who they are. She had the courage of her convictions and put personal integrity over income and security.

In generating loyalty from our customers and clients, we present ourselves as sales representatives, sales consultants, independent contractors, and business entrepreneurs, among other titles. In reality we might be more accurately described as hand holders, go-fers, enlighteners, and teachers. Robert Frost, the great poet laureate, said he was not so much a teacher as an awakener. Our job is to awaken our prospects and customers awareness of the benefits our product or service provides.

We can learn much about loyalty and customer service simply by watching how others interrelate with people. Comparison can be good for learning, but constantly comparing ourselves to others will prove to be nonmotivational as it eventually leads to arrogance or despair. We begin to think of ourselves as "so much better than" or "never being as good as" — both preoccupations are poison.

Find your giftedness and apply it in the field. They can teach a running back in football how to spin out of the grasp of a defender, or how to head fake in order to avoid a would-be tackler, but they cannot teach them *when* to do it. Some skills are instinctual. But there are a host of skills that anyone, regardless of their abilities, can practice in order to excel. For example, we mentioned in an earlier chapter the importance of knowing how to communicate. We live in a high-speed world today. Get to the bottom line as expediently as possible. The finesse comes when we can avoid having the prospect or customer feel like we're pushing them to a decision. Our mission, it seems to me, is to help people conduct their business more efficiently and effectively.

To find favor with both God and man, Proverbs 3:3 tells us to never forsake kindness and loyalty. If we're considerate and loyal to our customers in providing service, they will many times return the loyalty. This is known as physiological reciprocity. But don't be concerned if it doesn't come back to you from them; we often reap a harvest from a field different than the one in which we sowed. Do your best and let God do the rest.

Good Communication

Everyone likes to be listened to. The salespeople and companies who have the greatest loyalty among their customers are the ones who are good listeners. They know how to ask questions and then listen. The more we talk, the more we injure ourselves. This is so because the one who talks takes, and the one who listens gives. Most salespeople do too much taking. They talk when they feel a need to say something. Professional salespeople talk when they have something to say.

A possible reason so many salespeople talk too much is because they simply don't know when to stop talking. It's like the barber who doesn't know when to stop cutting someone's hair.

So the most important part of effective communication is listening. The biggest barrier to effective communication is the assumption that it has already taken place. It's the old thing of: I know you believe you understand what you think I said, but I'm not sure you realize that what you heard is not what I meant.

One way to insure clarity of communication is simply to ask. Not only do we need to ask qualifying questions that probe for needs, but also we need to ask questions to clarify a prospect's previous answers. Dave Floyd, a friend of mine in the real estate business, asks this closing question: "Are you folks convinced that this house meets your needs and will be a nice home for your family, or should I keep on selling?" He always asks this question with a soft non-threatening smile.

Doing Small Things Well

As you have probably already surmised, success in selling, business, or life itself, is a matter of doing many small things well. With this in mind, let's look at some small things that make a big difference regarding how Christ would have us serve.

It was Tony Campolo who said we are either into titles or into towels. If we are into titles we are into self, and if we are into self we slowly begin to die spiritually and emotionally. No less a person than Albert Einstein said that we are born to serve. Many individuals, along with many companies, give to get. This, of course, is self-serving. They look through lenses that focus on short-term gains rather than long-term returns.

Don't try to make a good impression on others, instead, look to serve others. In an age where the focus is on self, this can appear foolish. Self takes offense. A number of years ago a man came out of a lumber company in Phoenix, Arizona, to discover several men stealing lumber from his truck. He told them that it was his truck and offered to help them load it onto their truck. This man saw the bigger picture (Proverbs 25:21-22). He didn't see thieves, he saw men desperately in need of a Savior. He didn't see things through the eyes of owner-ship but through the eyes of provision. After they settled down, they asked him why he would do such a thing. His response was that he just wanted to show them the love of Jesus Christ in a practical way, i.e. by helping. As a result, a number of them received Jesus Christ as their Saviour .

Serving others even when they mean you harm is not only foolish but can be seen as outright stupidity in the eyes of a world held captive by deceptive philosophy. Remember, people without the Holy Spirit living in them do not accept the things of God, for the things of God are foolishness to them. They do not understand be-cause they cannot understand. Godly things are spiritu-ally discerned (Col. 2:8-10).

There's one other "small thing" that can make a difference — a guarded tongue. As salespeople we open our mouths to speak on the average of 700 times a day. Words are containers and hold either life, or fire and death (Prov. 15:1-4). They are weapons or tools. We are either demolition specialists or construction architects. We can neither control nor reverse the damage that words can do. The good impressions we try to make with our words can be effaced by a deceptive heart (James 3:9-12).

The Four Tongues

1). **The governed or bridled tongue.** This is the disciplined tongue and belongs to the person who puts their brain in gear before putting their mouth in motion. This person acts instead of reacts; they pause and carefully select their responses. And they have the maturity to keep their own counsel and not gossip with others.

2). **The concerned or regardful tongue.** The person with this tongue speaks truthfully (James 5:12). They seek to encourage. They will keep their word to their own hurt.

3). **The conniving tongue.** The person with this speech pattern is a schemer. They are filled with wrong motives and twist the truth. They're busybodies, gossips and badmouthers.

4). **The lawless tongue.** The possessor of this tongue is simply irresponsible and reckless. They are the quintessential "errant archer." You've seen them. Whether at the dinner table or a banquet table, given enough time, they will wound everyone present. These people can also be given to quick tempered words which can lead to rebellion and destruction (see Prov. 29:20).

Not only have sales been lost but careers ruined by one bad day, one careless remark. Like toothpaste out of the tube, we can't stuff those words back down our throats once they've escaped our lips. We can find ourselves paying the price for years because of a careless word or two.

To excel as a godly salesperson, we have seen that following the Golden Rule and treating our clients as we would want to be treated will help us become successful wherever we go or whatever we sell.

Chapter Five

Selling to Different Personality Types

I am sending you out like sheep among wolves. Therefore be as shrewd as snakes and as innocent as doves (Matthew 10:16)

To always look at the ideal and ignore reality will keep us forever tied to immaturity. Conversely, to only deal in reality and not reach for the ideal, will turn us into cynics.

If we venture into the marketplace looking through rose-colored lenses and humming *Kumbayah*, we'll be reduced to pulp in about three days. While most of our customers and clients are normal, nice people, there are some very nasty people out there. Some people will steal a hot stove if given half a chance.

Second Timothy 1:17 tells us not to be afraid of people, but to be wise and strong, loving and disciplined in our dealings with them. With that said, let's look at a number of personality types we will encounter in the real world. Remember, look for the best in people; be prepared for the worst; and let God take care of the rest. And try to have a thicker skin and a softer more compassionate heart.

The Egotist

The first type of person we'll look at is the egotist. Here's a key to understanding them: People with a low self-esteem will usually base their self-image on what they own, who they know, or what they can do. It doesn't take much imagination to picture the outcome if both prospect/customer/client and the sales representative suffer from poor self-image. At best the encounter will be reduced to seeing who can trump whom with stories of their troubles. At worst it will result in crossed sword points, alienation and lost business for your company. Remember, a client spends more money in repeat business than an initial customer. (Of course, you don't really work for your company at all, God is your general manager, so do your work as unto the Lord. Do your best and let God do the rest.)

Incidentally, there is a difference between pride and vanity. Vanity is inward directed manifesting itself in exaggerations, innocuous self-puffery, and overweening narcissism. This is all rather amusing stuff if we're secure in our own skin. As sexual sin appeals to an empty heart saying, "I need it," pride appeals to an empty head saying, "I deserve it." Pride is an insolent disdain directed towards others; it looks down a patrician nose in pietistic, tweedy condescension.

Our success in dealing with this type of customer then will depend on how secure we are. The majority of us would like to bring the egotist down. Here's the way to win over this type of customer and turn him or her into a client — discover the primary reason for their arrogance: is it their success, their position, their wealth?

A little flattery goes a long way with most people, but the egotist has an unending need for it. The objective is to remain pure of heart and resist the temptation to manipulate this prospect or customer through flattery. God never justifies the means to get to the end. Colossians 4:5-6 tells us to be wise in all of our contacts, to let our conversation be gracious as well as sensible, for then we will have the right answer for everyone.

The egotist has one quality that will serve you in dealing with him — egotistical people are almost always optimists. If you can endure their penchant for self-aggrandizement and listen to them, you will make sales that other salespeople will fail to make.

The Liar

The second type of prospect or customer we want to look at is particularly trying. We've all met him, he's the liar. Lying is such an insidious thing because it grows; small lies grow to more and bigger lies. Proverbs 28:6 says it is better to be poor and honest than rich and a liar.

The problem in dealing with a liar is that you never know where truth leaves off and lying takes over, so you're never quite sure where you stand. When dealing with a liar, skepticism is a wise ally. A discerning spirit will help you divide truth from falsehood. If it is inescapable that you deal with a liar, pray that the Lord will give you wisdom and understanding.

There are two ways to interact with the liar: Get everything in writing if at all possible. Secondly, repeat what the liar tells you for the purpose of confirmation: "You did say, didn't you___" "Am I understanding you to say___?" "You agree that this is the situation___."

Lying of course flies both ways, and we want to be absolutely unimpeachable in what we say. In James 5:12, it says to let our yes be yes and our no be no. Proverbs 6:17 tells us that pride and lying are among the seven abominations that the Lord hates. In Matthew 12:36-37 it says that we will have to give an account for every careless word we utter. So it behooves us to be careful in what we say ourselves and demand to have the customer's contract in writing.

The Negotiator

The next prospect/customer we encounter is the negotiator. These people thrive on getting concessions, especially when it comes to price. The problem is that once you concede on one point, they become like a piranha — they'll want to haggle about everything.

When I was preparing to write this book I worked at a national car dealership specializing in high quality used cars. This company has a fixed price policy that sets them apart from other dealerships. Most people, if not coming out of a Rip Van Winkle hibernation, are aware of this policy, yet people would still insist that they discount their prices. They had decided that somehow this national policy did not apply to them. This always struck me as unbelievable.

Here's how to best deal with the Negotiator, keeping in mind, their fundamental flaw — they're greedy. The Negotiator wants two things: to buy cheap, and receive "bragging rights." They want to be able to brag to others about what a terrific deal they got. To acquiesce on even the smallest point will bring on the negotiator's greed like a flood.

With this prospect/customer you need to build value; show them how much they'll save and what they'll gain. Talk in terms of dollars saved, and how good your product is. (Of course, do not make this claim if your product cannot stand the strain of use.)

The upside of dealing with this type of prospect/customer is once they realize you can't be bargained with, they become quite civilized and manageable and can even turn into loyal customers or clients.

The Cunning Prospect

Next we look at a type of prospect/customer most salespeople would rather avoid. But for the professional selling is much like Christianity in that we can't pick and choose what we'll accept. Moreover, we never want to put at risk the possibility of witnessing to these people sometime in the future. God puts people in our path to bless us or afflict us according to our needs. With that said, let me introduce you to the cunning prospect or customer. It is the extreme of shrewdness. (Remember, any strength taken to an extreme becomes a liability.)

A listing of synonyms for cunning will give you an idea of what you're up against when dealing with them: tricky, crafty, wily, shifty, Machiavellian. They are not above lying. It is best to keep these people in front of you and away from the light switches. This person's creed is: All is fair in love and war. Because of their greed they will take advantage of you in a heartbeat.

If you could view them from the profile, figuratively speaking, they'd be leaning into you at a 45 degree angle; always nudging, pushing, forcing. As with the Negotiator, make no concessions; they'll ambush you later in the sale with something you said or halfway promised. Make everything implicitly clear as you go along in the sales process; insert no ambiguity. Remember, they've been playing this game a long time. If you're not prepared to handle them correctly, they'll eat your lunch and take home the bag you brought it in.

If anything undersell this type of prospect or customer. Overselling is interpreted by them as eagerness or hunger and at that point, the jig is up. You won't realize you've been diced into a thousand pieces until you go to walk away. Also, with overselling you commit one of the cardinal sins of selling — you will talk too much. Talking too much in front of this type of prospect or customer will only mean laying a trap for yourself. This is the right place to remember the admonition: Brevity is power. The less said with this prospect, the better.

The one card you can play that the Cunning prospect or customer does not have is honesty. While you cannot hope to best this type of person at their game, you can remain safe as long as you remain honest and transparent. Two kinds of people will shy away from transparency — the insecure and the devious. But even these people will recognize and respect those possessing these character qualities.

The Cynical Prospect

Sarcastic or cynical prospects or customers are cutting and contemptuous, but in many cases they are smart people. They have a keen brain but their mind has not been redeemed, as Romans 12:2 talks about. Their tongues are swords. To the bone a true cynic is proud of their ability to reduce a fellow human being to pulp, and a salesperson is a special treat. If you're not prepared to handle this prospect or customer, it can be an unnerving experience indeed.

The key to handling this prospect/customer type is knowing that, although they can be quite smart, they almost always suffer from feelings of inferiority. Therein lies the clue to how to sell to this most difficult person. You obviously should never try to out match them, instead, listen and when you do respond, talk in a restrained tone and hopefully they will follow suit. Don't get all defensive and let your voice level get out of control.

If all of this does not bring about the desired results you

want, there is one response that almost never fails. It's called silence. Above all, handle the sarcastic or cynical type of customer with forbearance and self-control. You might even tell them that you didn't come to fight them, but to help them. It's pretty difficult for anyone to remain nasty when someone is genuinely trying to help them.

The Clam

The next prospect/customer type can strike us as a riddle wrapped in a mystery inside an enigma. This is the Clam. He doesn't talk but just sits there. Most salespeople, because they're gregarious and given to talking by their very nature, will fill the void. The Clam likes nothing better because as long as you're doing all the talking he can't be pinned down by having to make a decision.

The key to opening the Clam is to make him the central figure on stage. Build your whole presentation around him. Ask him questions that cannot be answered with a simple yes or no. Any question beginning with "who, what, where, why, or when demands an explanatory answer. If he somehow still seems to remain taciturn, there is one strategy that almost never fails. Solicit their opinion or suggestions. Almost no human being is impervious to the flattery of having their opinion sought after.

The Forceful Prospect

The forceful prospect or customer is most often a large person, and they are predominantly males. The late President Lyndon Johnson is a prime example. He would use his height when buttonholing a colleague and lean over them; it was very intimidating for most. The Forceful prospect/customer is somewhat of a browbeater and can easily become a full blown bully. But you can sell this person. Not only can you sell them, you can turn them into a steadfast and loyal customer. Again, like any other personality type we've met in our gallery, you never want to take them on. Remember they've been practicing for years to be the way they are. The key here is to let this prospect sell himself. Show deference and respect — which we should with everyone — because this person is most often found in a top management position. Not often found to be a clear thinker, they are, as General Robert E. Lee described John Bell Hood, all lion and no fox. But go ahead and compliment them on their assertiveness and astuteness.

By his very nature the Forceful prospect prides him or herself on "buying," never being sold. A key here then is to give them many reasons why you're making the suggestions you're making. After this plethora of positive points for purchasing, sit back and fall silent. In most cases they'll ponderously come to embrace your suggestions.

The Procrastinator

If you're in a fast-paced industry, this person will be the bain of your existence. They seem to have three speeds: slow, slower, and "oh I've got a headache." They deliberate, meditate, ponder, and ruminate; you're hoping this sale will go down before the second coming happens.

Again, their nature tells you how to sell them. One of their fears is the fear of loss: loss of money, time, or profit through a poor decision. With most of us the fear of loss outstrips the possibility of gain. Most of us will scramble harder to save $100 than we will to make a it. So, especially with this prospect or customer, you wave the possibility of loss before him, loss that almost certainly will happen if they do not move on the deal now. This is especially effective if you can show the prospect with pencil and paper how this will happen.

You might also use the old Churchillian strategy of complimenting them on a characteristic you wish them to have. Compliment them, for example, on being wise in weighing the pros and cons and then moving ahead as other sensible people have done.

The Talker

This prospect is a verbal fire hydrant. They are perfectly capable of opening the conversation, providing the body of the conversation, and closing it. The uninitiated will find themselves in a revolving door and out on the street before they can gather their wits about them.

The problem with the Talkative prospect or customer is exactly the opposite of what you faced with the Clam. As you cannot "out power" the Forceful prospect, you cannot "out talk" the Talker. The thing that will prove fatal to your sales effort here is to show impatience.

Anyone can bulldoze; it's all elbows and that takes no talent. While this works for some high pressure sales-people, they are destined to enjoy short-term gains while missing out on long-range profits. But those pro-fessional salespeople who sell with finesse lead their prospects or customers to a successful conclusion. How we lead them, obviously varies according to their per-sonality type.

With the Talker you use a device called "Capping." You let them babble on until there's a break in the conversa-tion or they come to a point where you want to interject something; get the cart back on the right set of rails. The idea is to channel their remarks onto a course of conver-sation you wish to pursue. "Capping" is nothing more than summing up their remarks, then going off in the di-rection you wish to go. Do not use this tool prematurely, or it will be perceived as a brush-off.

Here is your silver bullet to use with the Talker prospect or customer. It's just five simple words: "You said something just then." Or maybe, "Now that's an interesting point you just made." Deep down in their soul, the Talker knows they haven't said anything interesting in over a year! They'll stop abruptly to see just what it was you noticed that was so interesting. Don't be concerned about a connection between what they think you noticed and what you have to say; the idea is to break their unending flow of blather. Focus is not their forte and they will soon be caught up in the new conversational direction and will not press the point.

The Angry Customer

The first rule in dealing with an angry customer is never to argue or defend yourself. You cannot deal rationally with someone who's emotionally bouncing off the ceiling and ricocheting off walls. Let them "air-out." Never change the expression on your face, which should be one of composure and stoicism. Obviously if you or your company is at fault, admit it and make every attempt to correct it. The whole point of confrontation is to settle the issue and get back to a productive relationship.

As I've said, let them air-out and when they've finished, calmly say "Is that all? Is there anything else we need to address while we're together?" They might have more need to ventilate, and if so, let them go. When they've spent themselves on this second round of vitriol, say something like, "Anything else, Mr. Martin?" The point in all of this is to get them to drop their octave, getting back down on terra firma, regaining some semblance of rationality, some vestige of normalcy. You cannot deal with people who are emotionally out of control.

All-in-all we want to make every attempt to avoid these kinds of distasteful encounters. There's a Proverb that says it is easier to take a defended city than to win back an offended person.

The Timid Prospect

This shy person would be quite comfortable living in a closet. Almost obsequious, it takes them all day to get through the queue at the bank or grocery store because they keep letting everyone else go ahead of them. Almost apologetic for using up too much oxygen, they try to become invisible. At a party or dinner gathering you will find them in a corner somewhere.

The great temptation for salespeople when encountering this prospect or customer is to think: I've been lied to by the Liar, resigned to silence by the Forceful or Talkative prospect, driven to near madness by the Procrastinator, pushed around, abused, treated like a third-class citizen, but this one's mine! Resist the inclination to browbeat this person. They do have a soul and an ego.

Here's the key to dealing with this type of prospect or customer. Keep in mind that nobody solicits or values their opinion. This is your silver bullet: Speak a little more slowly with this prospect; avoid giving them the impression that you're putting your hands to the small of their back and rushing them up the mountain to a decision. Be respectful, for they don't get much of that either. Give more detailed explanations and ask for their thoughts as you go along. If treated right, these people will become some of your most loyal clients. Oh, and one more important point about the Timid prospect or customer, they are usually more sensitive than most prospect types you'll deal with, so be very careful to keep all commitments and promises to the letter.

Well, we've looked at some of the personality types we'll encounter along the way; space here does not allow us to explore them all. Remember two important things as we leave this chapter. Many prospects think that the salesman's attitude is: Mr. or Mrs. Buyer, you have my money in your pocket and my objective is to get my money out of your pocket and into my bank account. Regretfully this is true with some. This salesperson loves money and things and uses people. The idea is to love people by respecting them and having their best interests at heart.

The second thing we want to keep in mind is so very important. If we are ambassadors for the King of kings then we must always be on the alert for an opening to tell them about our King. If they see a dichotomy between what we say and what we do it will foul any future opportunities we might have to witness to them. Martin Luther said there are two days: today and that day. We want to avoid at all costs having them come up to us on that day and say, as they step to the left, "Why didn't you tell me about your Jesus?"

Chapter Six

The 30-Day Makeover

How to Revolutionize Your World

Lord, put me in the center of your assignment for my life.

One time when I flew into a major city in Australia to give a presentation, I saw a funny thing as I joined a group of people to wait for cabs. A dog with one eye walked by and someone in the group said, "Look at that dog with one eye!" Five people cover one eye and watched that dog as it ambled on by. I thought to myself, *I know a lot of people like that, just ambling through life, always getting ready to live but never really living; always getting ready to commence to begin to get started perhaps maybe tomorrow in living their lives and capturing their dreams!*

Have you ever noticed how good things just seem to happen to certain people, and other people, good, honest, hard working people, never seem to get any higher on the mountain in their quest for significance? On they go through silent pain, no closer at 60 than they were at 30 or 40 in achieving their purpose in life, destined it seems to die terminally frustrated or perplexed about life.

The reason fulfilling our purpose is so very vital is that it brings glory to God, and everything created is for the express purpose of bringing glory to God.

Hopefully in this chapter we will be able to clear up some of the mystery as to why some people make it and some fall short, but if we don't, at least you'll be confused on a higher level.

After I got out of the military and completed my higher education — I did not graduate — I went to work for my father who owned the largest real estate company in northwestern Ohio. My father told my twin brother and I that because we were the sons of the owner, we only had to work half days...and he didn't care which 12 hours it was either.

After several years of selling in the field, I was promoted to management. It didn't take me long to learn that there's a great difference between looking successful and being successful. And by successful I'm talking about the use of our gifts, talents, and abilities to live lives of passion, purpose, and power!

God deposited in each one of us a "genetic promise." In Jeremiah 29:11 it says, "For I know the plans that I have for you, plans to prosper you and not to harm you, plans to give you hope and a future."

In building my office of 22 long ball hitters, I interviewed over 200 sales candidates. I observed an interesting thing in all those interviews; no one ever told me that it was their burning ambition in life to be the greatest failure their family ever produced. We all want to achieve a sense of purpose.

How does it happen then? Why is it that so many of God's people seem to be eating the peel and throwing away the banana? Well, someone's figured out the answer to that. Most people, it would seem, never miss an opportunity to miss an opportunity, all caught up in the thick of thin things. They'll spend more time talking about the news, sports, and weather than thinking about what God's purpose is for their life.

We don't drift to success, but we most assuredly can drift to failure. It was Miguel de Cervantes who said, "By the streets of bye and bye, one arrives at the house of never!" If we don't take a serious look at the Man in the

The 30-Day Makeover

Mirror, as Patrick Morley talks about in his book by the same name, we're no better off than the neighbor's cat!

Some people will never find their purpose in life because they're preoccupied living vicariously through others, e.g., movie stars or sports figures. They get all excited watching others earn an excellent living by throwing a ball, bouncing a ball, serving a ball, driving a ball, rolling a ball, or kicking a ball, while they wile away their lives sitting in that $100,000 a year chair in front of their 52 square foot, flat screen, surround-sound, wall T.V. Excitement without a purpose is just a spasm! It's merely moving the dust around!

Oswald Chambers in his classic book, *My Utmost for His Highest*, said, "Don't waste your life by giving yourself to an inferior purpose." You could take any subject — world history, investing wisely in mutual funds, the Bible — and study everything you can find on that subject. At the end of 30 days, you would know more about that topic than 95% of the people alive in the world today! You could do that with your job or your ministry!

Studs Terkle, the Nobel Prize winning author, said, "I believe that people today are looking for a calling and not just a job." I have found that a person with a calling will always outwork, out earn, or outlast the person who merely works out of a sense of duty!

We are either fishing in life or merely maintaining an aquarium. Some people are like the Dead Sea, always taking in but never giving anything out. In the workplace there are those who stand on the curbstones and critique; others step off the curbstones into the street and move progressively towards a worthwhile objective. In the church setting they sit in the pews waiting for the second coming. We need to get out of the pews and into our purpose; out of maintenance and into mission.

The Makeover

If you want to live a life of passion, purpose, and power, to really soar, I want you to try an experiment that will last 30 days. It will revolutionize your life! I call it the 30-day makeover. Remember, choices not chance or luck determine our destiny. Don't begin your 30-day experiment until you're determined to persevere.

Now your experiment won't be easy, but the great prizes in life are always in direct proportion to the resistance. God never said the way would be easy or inexpensive. He did not promise a calm passage, only a safe arrival.

In your 30-day experiment get a vivid picture in your mind of the kind of person you would like to be. See yourself doing the things that person would do. With the help of the Holy Spirit to form your heart, transform your mind, and conform your will, your actions will catch up with your picture. If you change your actions before changing your picture, you will keep going back to what's familiar. This is why New Year's resolutions don't work; we lose our picture or vision.

Write out a description of the kind of person you would like to be. Writing forces us to think in concrete, specific terms, rather than in general, vague terms. Your written description of the person you want to become now becomes your focus. Your outlook on life should never be determined by circumstances, but by focus. The picture you have of yourself, either positive or negative, becomes your "compass setting," guiding you inexorably towards its fulfillment.

In the Bible, in Proverbs 23:7 it says, "For as a man thinketh within himself, so is he." Our life is shaped by our thoughts. Our society places a great emphasis on training the brain. Romans 12:2 says, however, not to be conformed to the time of life in which you live, but be transformed by the renewing of you brain? No! It's not our brain that needs to be renewed, it's our mind!

During your 30-day experiment, watch how you talk to yourself. We spend 80-85% of our time thinking or talking to ourselves. We do this in the morning when we're getting ready for work, driving, or waiting in line. Most people let their mind control them by thinking in critical, judgmental terms rather than in creative, positive terms. The creative mind produces an idea while the average mind produces a verdict.

Here's a question to ask yourself in the private court-room of your own mind: "If I had a friend who talked to me the way I talk to me, would I associate with them? The idea is to keep your thoughts from running riot. Shut off the negative! You need to give up in order to move up! "I wish," "If only," "I can't," and "I'll never," are staples in the vocabulary of the failing. This kind of negative self-talk serves only to program your mind for self-fulfilling prophecy. Negative self-talk causes low ex-pectations; low expectations result in low yield!

If you choose to do your 30-day experiment don't be surprised by resistance. This resistance will usually come from those closest to you. Their first reaction will be one of disbelief. The next level of their resistance comes in the form of "helping you" to save yourself from yourself as it were. They will appeal to common sense reasoning, e.g. "You've tried something like this in the past," "We didn't raise you to think like this," "You don't have the right education." If all this fails to deter you, they will resort to something few of us can withstand for long — criticism or rejection.

Somewhere, sometime, if we ever hope to live with pas-sion, purpose, and power, we have to stop asking "What will others think?" and begin asking, "What is the right

thing for me to do?" Opportunity is sometimes spelled...
R.I.S.K. And risk is sometimes spelled...F.O.O.L.I.S.H.
Sometimes we have to be willing to "stand alone," to
risk looking foolish in the eyes of others. Right can
never be determined by numbers.

During your 30-day experiment, go about your day with
a quiet assurance, knowing that you must reap what you
sow; it may take awhile, but as sure as the sun comes up
in the east and settles in the west, it will come to pass.
In fact, there is no way that it cannot, for it's one of the
immutable laws we talked about earlier. "Everything in
nature, even dust and feathers go by laws and not by
luck," Emerson said, "and what we sow so shall we
reap." These laws apply to all people equally everywhere
and have since the dawn of human history! We need
only to work in harmony with these laws and believe.

Give of yourself during your 30-day experiment like
you've never done before; do more than is expected of
you. Life is like a game of tennis you: the person who
serves well seldom loses. You can drive down any street
in America and tell which businesses are giving the best
service. And don't be concerned about where your return will come from; we often reap a wonderful harvest
from a field different than the one in which we've sown.
This is another one of those laws we talked about, The
Law of Mutual Exchange. As surely as we reap what we
sow, so we cannot help others to prosper without pros-

pering ourselves. You might have heard this law contemporarily expressed as, "We get back what we give out," or "What goes around comes around."

In Luke 6:38, it says: "If you give, you will get! Your gift will return to you in full and overflowing measure, pressed down, shaken together to make room for more. Whatever measure you use to give — large or small — will be used to measure what is given back to you." This law applies to everyone. There are good, unredeemed people using this law to their advantage and yet do not understand that it is a universal law. Other Christians understand this principal yet fail to use it.

Karl Menninger, founder of the Menninger Clinic (an international psychiatric center), said that he could not remember having ever treated a generous person. Goethe, early 19th century poet, dramatist, and philosopher said, "They who do nothing for others, do nothing for themselves." Your soul is nourished when you give; it is injured when you are self-centered.

In your experiment, try loving people and using money and things, rather than loving money and things and using people for 30 days. Einstein said, "We are born to serve." In the Bible it says, "The greatest among you must be the servant of all." But servanthood is tough cheese in a self-serving society whose gospel is "Me first!"

Now, don't worry during your 30-day experiment. Worry-driven people are controlled by circumstances and the fear of failure. Failure looks back; worry looks around; faith and trust look ahead. You cannot stress and trust at the same time. Refuse to let the clouds of yesterday or the apprehensions about tomorrow, dim your prospects for today.

Four things will prevent you from mounting up with wings like eagles:

1. FEAR. We are born with only two fears: The fear of falling and the fear of loud noises; every other fear is acquired! Fear is the adversary that keeps us from achieving the good we might win. Fear keeps our dreams at a distance!

2. CONFUSION. With confusion we don't know who's right or what's right. The result is that we head off in our own direction. There is a way, the Scriptures tell us, that seem right to a man, but in the end it is death. This can be emotional death, physical death, or spiritual death. If light is consistently rejected we will end in total darkness.

3. PERFECTIONISM. Perfectionism will keep us pecking with the chickens instead of soaring with the eagles. It is better to be effective than to be perfect. Perfectionists — nit-pickers drive other people crazy! The cure for per-

fectionism is something called, "Calculated Neglect." By our wills we purpose to leave the picture crooked, refrain from turning down the collar of total strangers, refuse to pick hair or lint from others' clothing. I used to be a perfectionist, but I've been delivered. Hallelujah! Now if I see someone walking out of the restaurant with their napkin still tucked into their pants, I let them walk right on by. I no longer feel obligated to save the world from embarrassing moments.

4. BUSYNESS The fourth thing that will rob you of God's best for your life is shunning the discipline of solitude. Constantly doing, rarely reflecting, we get caught up in the vortex of busyness. This causes people to miss a life filled with meaning. We need to relax, have a little fun and invest some time and money in memories.

Once you complete your 30-day experiment, it is vitally important that you surround yourself with like-minded people. You must find a group of people that care enough about you to be honest with you, for only in transparency is there light, and only in light is there life and growth!

In Proverbs, it says: "You have no friend or ally in someone who will not share a truth, and better wounds from a friend than kisses from an enemy." Truth without judgment is truth that sets free! In the end, Proverbs 28:23 tells us that people appreciate frankness more than flattery. Only a fool wants to continually hear the echo of their own voice.

Your group of "right thinking" people can become your Mind Trust. In the book of Ecclesiastes it says, "Two or three are better than one; if one falls, their friends can help them up. But pity the one who falls and has no one to help them up." We need others to help us endure. This is one reason why the church is so very important, Ephesians 2:19 tells us.

Knowledge is knowing what to do; wisdom is knowing how to do it; virtue is doing it! But we must do it right. To be lawless and do our own thing is to slip through the crack in our soul into the hell of self without God, as Leanne Payne talks about in her book, *Crisis in Masculinity*. To refuse to do it God's way is to fall like an egg from a tall chicken.

Playwright Eugene O'Neill said, "If the human race is so senseless that in 2000 years it hasn't had the brains to appreciate that the secret of happiness is contained in one simple sentence, which you'd think any school kid could understand and apply, then it's time we dumped it down the drain and let the ants have a chance. That simple sentence is: 'For what shall it profit a man if he gains the whole world and suffers the loss of his own soul.'"

As I've said, don't start your 30-day experiment until you're determined to persevere. Then do your 30-day experiment, repeat it, then repeat it again until it becomes a part of your core values. You get into it, and then it gets into you. Once it does, you'll wonder how you ever lived any other way!

If you fail during your 30-day experiment, that is, if you become overwhelmed and discouraged and want to go back your old way of thinking, you must start over and go another 30 days. Do your best; prepare for the worst; and let God do the rest. He tells us that He will finish a good work which He has started.

Thinking about perseverance I can't help but think of the story about the reporter who asked the prizefighter, "What kind of fighter are you?" The fighter said, "I'm always up...or getting up!" When he was knocked to the canvas, in his mind, he was getting up! We need to be like that fighter.

Pay the price; do it right. The Bandit dreams of all he can get; the Builder dreams of all he can do. Those who consistently try to take shortcuts in life delude themselves, becoming conspirators to their own undoing. They lie in ambush for their own lives.

The streets where the broken walk are filled with those who thought they could do it their way. They may succeed for a while, but nature tolerates no long-term robberies. There is a Judge whose eyes never close in sleep, who cannot be bribed nor deceived. They eat the better fruit of their own ways, and fade away In their pursuits. Jeremiah 17:11 says, "Like a partridge that hatches eggs it did not lay, so are they who make gains by unjust means; it will leave them in the midst of their days, and in the end they will prove to be a fool."

Do you want to live with passion, purpose, and power? Do you want to be rich and have joy as you go through life? If you do it God's way, your riches will far exceed any amount of earthly riches you could ever hope to amass, for earthly riches are tied to present value, and values change! No, your riches will be something that can never be taken from you — the contentment that comes not from "what" you know, but "Who" you know! Not in "who" you are, but in "Whose" you are!

In closing this chapter I would like to tell you a story about an old carpenter who decided to retire; he wished to spend more time working around the house and doing the things he'd longed to do.

The contractor was obviously sorry to see his valued and highly skilled worker go and asked if he would stay on for just one more house, as a personal favor. The carpenter agreed, but soon shoddy workmanship and the use of inferior materials gave evidence that his heart was no longer in his work. It was a sad note on which to end a stellar career — 30 years of faithful service. When he had finished his work and the contractor came by to inspect the house, he handed the front door keys to the carpenter. "This is your house," he said, "my gift to you."

What a shock! What a shame! If only he had known he was building his own house, he would have done things so differently. And so it is with us. We build our lives in a distracted way. At important points we fail to give our best effort. Then one day we realize with dismay that we are now living in the house we have built.

Think of yourself as the carpenter. Each day you place a board, hammer a nail, or erect a wall, build wisely; it is the only life you will ever build. A plaque says it all, "Life is a do-it-yourself project." Your life today is the result of your attitudes and choices in the past. Your life tomorrow will be the result of the attitudes and choices you make today!

God determines what we may become; we decide what we shall become. The Bible says, "I set before you today life or death, so choose life in order that you might live." From birth to age 19 is the springtime of life; 19 to age 38 is the summer of life; 38 to 57 represents the fall season of life; and 57 and beyond is the winter season of our life. It is never too late to grow! I challenge you to make your own 30-day experiment.

Chapter Seven

The Little Things That Make Big Things Happen

Paying Vast Attention to Details

There's a story about a very successful businessman pointing to his framed PhD hanging on the wall of his office. He tells a friend, "That cost me two wives and three children." Then with sad reflection he added, "No one has ever commented on my PhD."

I know of another man who lived in a downtown hotel in my hometown — a multimillionaire, divorced, alienated from his children, able to eat only very small portions of food due to having had half his stomach removed. I often wondered if he had any regrets on Thanksgiving and Christmas as he sat alone in his hotel suite.

The Scriptures tell us to count the cost before we build. We will live with the consequences of our actions. We should ponder with due diligence exactly what we are willing to pay for success, and exactly how that success is defined. The accumulation of things or the accolades of mere men can be hollow indeed.

Anyone who has been in selling any length of time can tell you that success doesn't come from doing one or two major things well; it's a matter of doing a host of little things well. As one of my mentors used to say, "Vast attention to details, John, vast attention to details."

In this chapter we will look at a number of little things that in and of themselves will not make or break our chances for excellence, but collectively, will enable us to achieve purpose and significance.

One reason that there is really very little competition today is that most people want to take the line of least resistance; get by, as Huxley said, with the least amount of discredit.

We've all looked at someone who seems to have it all together and asked ourselves what it is about them that makes them so different. Let me assure you they did not come by their ability naturally. While it can be said with assurance that some people have greater aptitude than others, there is no such thing as a natural born salesman. Like there are no natural born physicians, scientists, or skilled auto-mechanics, highly effective salespeople have acquired and honed their skills.

One of the most successful insurance salesmen in the country and I were participating in a large sales congress together, and he told the audience that he felt selling was 2% product knowledge and 98% people knowledge. Another speaker and mentor of mine used to refer to the importance of people skills in selling as "Human Engineering." We do have to know how people work.

People not only listen to what we say, they watch what we do. David Henry Thoreau said, "What you do thunders so loudly in my ears I cannot hear what you are saying." If, for example, we tell a customer or client (remember, we want to take our customers to client status because they do repeat business with us) that we will meet them at a certain time and we fail to be there on time, the message we send the customer or client is, "Whatever I was doing was more important than being on time for you!" Keep in mind, the customer is the profit, and we're the overhead! Shakespeare said punctuality is a compliment to the intelligent and an insult to the unintelligent. Today, with the availability of cell phones, almost any excuse for failing to extend the courtesy of a call holds no water.

All human relationships are based on needs being met.

Human need is the point of contact. Mutual benefit is the ideal. We hear the expression, win/win situations. Unfortunately, because of greed or pride, this mutual success can break down. When one of the players comes out second best, their response is usually retaliatory. If the customer or client is the one coming out second best, they simply stop doing business with you. No opportunity is lost in business; your competition will take it. It's five times easier to take care of and keep an existing customer/client than it is to secure a new one. Economically it's prudent to take precautions.

Building Effective Relationships

There are five progressive steps in building an effective relationship:

1) Introduction. In the selling realm this is your initial approach. Remember, the eyes are a camera lens, the mind a film, and there's no re-take with a first impression.

2) Presenting of facts. This is comprised of chit-chat in order to establish common ground. In this phase you're trying to take the measure of the person you're working with.

3) Expressing points of view or dispensing advice or counsel.

4) Sharing impressions, empathies, or true reactions or feelings.

5) Truth. The sooner we can get to level five the more quickly we establish trust.

One of the things we want to avoid at all costs is of course, wrecking what we've labored to build. The pathway to broken relationships also happens in five stages.

1). The first step is a hurt or a wound. This can happen as a result of customer neglect, broken promises or commitments. In some cases even the perception of a slight or transgression can cause the loss of a customer. We live in an age of thin-skinned people. Some customers or clients are so high maintenance that the time you're taking to nurse them would be better spent investing in three new prospective customers. The time/value ratio says, Is what I'm doing now worth the time it's taking to do it? If not you might want to consider sending this customer to your competition.

2) Anger on the part of the offended customer or client

3) Anger escalates to resentment

4) Resentment turns into animosity

5) Animosity spirals into indifference. Salespeople who have perfected the art of alienating customers and clients have skinny kids.

A skilled salesperson knows how to wield a double-edged sword. One side of the sword blade is truth, the other respect. One transgression that even Christian salespeople seem to make over and over is something we discussed earlier — promising short but delivering long. This profanes truth. I believe it is done because of pressure: pressure to make quota; pressure to beat out a competitor; or even time pressure. Broken promises tear apart trust. This is tantamount to dismantling your own house board by board.

If you can't perform the service or deliver the product in the allotted time specified, be straitforward and honest and tell the customer or client the truth. If your service or product has superior benefits, build value until the customer sees the advantage in waiting for it. If you cannot truthfully say your service or product has advantageous benefits, perhaps you should entertain the thought of going to work for the company that has them. It's difficult to be the best when you're not working for the best.

We all go through life with a bank of imaginary buttons on our tummy. There's an "Empathy" button, an "Eager" button, a "Compassionate" button, a "Frustrated" button, a "Happy" button, and an "Anger" button, all neatly lined up like the buttons on the face of a telephone. The longer we're around another person, the more certain we are as to where these buttons are located. We know exactly where our mate's buttons are. For example, if I take food at the dinner table and fail to pass it along and soon have all the food gathered around my plate. I know that my dear bride is going to lift off like a Titan rocket. I must admit, sometimes I will just test her. Now her dropping toothpaste in the sink and letting it harden is another matter.

When we're dealing with an irate customer or one whose only job is to spread ignorance, it's beneficial to keep in mind the wise counsel our dear ancestors imparted to us: count to ten. This is also known as, "pause-and-select." Pause and select is the proper response or maybe the proper response is no response at all. Sometimes we're too quick to defend ourselves. If they are trying to punch our button for whatever reason, it seems best to remember the adage: Love your adversary and it will completely confuse them.

If you watch television comedy shows — you will notice today it's all about the "put-down." This may be innocuous fodder for television programs, but it is death in business encounters. Words are containers and hold either life or death. We cannot always agree or oblige, but we can always speak obligingly. Remember, the one who angers you controls you.

As I've mentioned, we are a nation of thin-skinned people. It is referred to as "taking offense." People have left a church over the color of the bulletin. For 20 years the Easter bulletin had been lavender, now some new "young bloods" decided to have them in rose. Or, the music's too loud. We're not singing the old hymns that we've been singing for 45 years. People take offense more quickly today. We have to be a great deal more diplomatic than ever before.

Appearance

We should look as well in dress as the best dressed person we will call on — otherwise that person will discount us to a certain extent. We also need to pay careful attention to the words you use. I've said before that words are containers and that when we speak our minds are on parade; not only our minds, but our hearts as well. The Bible says that what's in the heart of man comes forth from his mouth. We must think before we speak. We must put our brain in gear before we put our mouths in motion. Some people speak when they feel a need to say something; other people speak when they have something to say. God bless the person who, having nothing to say, remains silent. If one remains silent, Proverbs tells us, those around us will believe us to be wise.

Words do have power so we must be careful that we

don't use them to manipulate. There are words that will be most effective to open your presentation. There are attention grabbing words, words that appeal, exciting and stimulating words, informative words, powerful words, reliable words, words that are clinchers, persuasive words, words that enhance a companies image, words to justify a higher price, words to sell yourself, words to marginalize your competition. Words are powerful. I would suggest that you invest in a copy of *Words That Sell* by Richard Bayan, Contemporary Books, a division of McGraw-Hill Companies.

How to Conduct Oneself

Another area of critical importance is how to conduct oneself at a "Power Lunch." John Molloy found in a survey conducted a number of years ago that roughly 60% of corporate executives would never consider letting someone who does not know how to conduct themselves at the table, represent their company. Remember, when you're out with clients, you are the company.

The rules for good manners and civility apply at the table as well as anywhere else. People of any status will judge your socioeconomic background by things like how much you move your arm when eating. Sophisticated people move their wrist with as little movement as possible. Flying elbows or gesturing with your utensils will cause alarm at best, and at worst, can cause injury to those seated near you.

Most people are capable of starting off well but once things get going and they become relaxed, they lapse back into their normal pattern of eating. Waiting to learn good manners until you need to know is like waiting until you're under fire to prepare your shells on the front lines, by the time you engage it's over; judgment has been passed.

We have lost much of our eloquence and our elegance today. We neither know how to speak well or dress well. We are a casual society and while that has certain advantages in breaking down stiff formality, it can cause laxness. One place where this is most evident is at the dining table. One major transgression is talking with a mouth full of food. The opera diva, Leontyne Price, had some wise thoughts to offer along these lines. Whenever she was being interviewed over lunch for a perspective operatic role, she always ordered white fish. She would take small bites and in that way, she said, if asked a question, she could swallow without choking or have to talk with a mouth full of food. Trying to eat and talk at the same time is an egregious breech of good manners, and speaks volumes about one's lack of social graces.

Here then is a short list of additional transgressions that could cause you to be spending much time eating alone: The finer the restaurant the greater the importance of refraining from straws and chocolate milk. Bring your food up to your mouth; it's mind numbing the number of people who seem to have their forearm glued to the table. Never attempt to do two things at one time, e.g. pick up your water glass and reach for a roll. Speaking of rolls, you tear rolls, you never cut them.

Limited, precise movements and small bites are an indication of an educated, urbane person. Try to avoid looking like you haven't eaten in days; small portions please. Avoid comments like, "Boy, this stuff sure looks good!" Keep conversation at a low level, the people at the other end of the table shouldn't be able to hear every word you say. The luncheon or dinner table is not meant for a public address.

Dropping things on the table or yourself is to be carefully avoided, unless you're an octogenarian, in which case you've probably earned the right to carry on. If you should be so unfortunate as to drop something under the table, with the possible exception of your Mont Blanc fountain pen, do not go chasing after it. If peas are served or you decide to take some from the buffet table, don't feel compelled to consume every last little one.

Finally, don't slump in your chair, hold both utensils in the same hand, leave your fork or spoon in your dessert bowl or dish, unbuckle your belt, pick your teeth, rock back in your chair, or wipe your mouth with anything other than a napkin. These mark one as lacking in gastronomical propriety and destined to eat in dimly lit rooms behind closed doors.

Male and Female Conduct

When we as sales representatives are in the arena, in the heat of the sale, it is very easy for us to lose our perspective. If we are female we may tend to use our feminine wiles. Most men are too obtuse and lacking in sagacity to see this coming. Most men are easy prey for this ploy.

Men will resort to "sweet-talk." After all that's one of the reasons they are in sales, they know how to talk. These subtle traps become gaping snares if one is blessed with good looks. The more handsome, the more self-assured, the more successful we are, the greater the trip wire. Pride goes before a fall. Satan moves from the flesh, to the mind, to the spirit. God moves from the spirit, to the mind, to control of the flesh. The deceitfulness of sexual sin is in its perception; what is gained from a moment of passion is perceived, what is lost is real and permanent. The truth is that we cannot separate conduct from character, we will act out who we are. In the next chapter we will look at how we become the person God really wants us to be.

The demon behind power is pride. True power liberates and sets free. It has been said that power corrupts and absolute power corrupts absolutely. Convoluted power dominates; redeemed power serves. Where the power of money strikes at the wallet, and the power of sex hits below the belt, power leads us to believe we are right.

We lust to lord it over others. Power mixed with pride devastates relationships because it destroys dialogue.

Money can be a subtle and dominating master. Sex, like a river overflowing its banks, wants satisfaction not counsel. Power is heady wine and leads to pride. Uncontrollable sex is the result of an empty heart. Pride is the result of an empty head.

Now, let's take a look at the One who can heal broken hearts, deliver the captives, and set at liberty those who are bruised. The One who deeply loves us, believes in us, and desperately wants to see us become all that we are supposed to be.

Chapter Eight

The Advocate

Defender, Supporter,
Justifier, Counselor

Helen Keller, the great benefactor of the blind was once asked if there was anything worse than being without sight. She replied, "To have sight but lack vision." This remarkable woman who missed seeing shimmering sun sets, the splendor of meadows dressed in spring flowers, the beauty of a thoroughbred at full stride, saw things through the eyes of her heart that cannot be perceived by the natural eye. "Poor eyes," Bible scholar Franklin Fields said, "limits your sight; poor vision limits your deeds."

Glaucoma is a sad disease of the eyes in which a person's peripheral vision closes in until they are alone in darkness. This same thing can happen to a person spiritually. By getting all caught up in the excitement of the chase and the thrill of the deal, we become oblivious to the real purpose of life. There is a way that seems right to a man, a proverb goes, but in the end it is death. Sometimes the problem isn't in failing but in succeeding in the wrong areas. Success isn't always about what we do, but how we do it, and what we leave behind. There are children who will be the subject of whispers their entire lives because of the foolishness of their fathers. A good reputation is better than great riches.

God doesn't delight in what is big or great. He rejoices in what is right. Men have been elevating themselves by erecting edifices displaying their power and glory since the tower of Babel. Might-makes-right is not a biblical concept. The confident strides of a prideful person will be shortened.

In the last chapter I mentioned that success isn't a matter of doing one or two major things well, but a matter of doing a number of small things correctly. In many cases it is the little foxes that steal the grapes. It's what I call, tripping over trifles. What kind of madness causes a person, sane in every other sense, to hurl down a super-highway at speed, facing sudden death in the form of oncoming traffic, without buckling their seat belt? Yet, good people, smart people, do this every day spiritually.

Spiritual carelessness causes "death in slow doses," and it can be worse than sudden death. For a person to watch their life ebb away as they self medicate with the potions & snake oils this world has to offer is a tragedy beyond expression. This sadness is compounded when the one wasting away is a Christian — we who are supposed to be more than conquerors and living victoriously. There is something incomprehensibly askew when a Christian commits suicide, either physically, emotionally, or spiritually. Of the three, I believe spiritual suicide to be the most difficult to discern. Like kudzu, the fast growing vine introduced into this country in the mid 19th century for the control of erosion, spiritual erosion comes upon us gradually until, like kudzu, it smothers everything else in our life.

Sales people face rejection every day, and rejection can pinch off a little bit of our spirit until we are in full blown discouragement or even depression. Whether the rejection is personal or simply a disinterest in our product or service, it can wound as mortally as bullets or shrapnel on a battlefield. To try and maintain emotional and spiritual equilibrium on our own is impossible and foolish. But there is a helper, a supporter, one who sticks closer than a brother, and He is our Advocate.

The enemy, the one who prowls about like a lion seeking someone to devour, is out to suck the joy and excitement for life right out of your soul. Many years ago it was announced that the devil was thinking about going out of business and would sell all his equipment to those who were willing to pay the price. On the big day of the sale, all his tools were attractively displayed. There was Envy, Jealousy, Hatred, Malice, Deceit, Prejudice, Pride, Gossip, Idolatry and other implements on display. Each tool was marked with its own price tag.

Over in the corner by itself was a rather harmless looking tool, very much worn, yet it bore a higher price tag than any of the others. Someone asked the devil what it was, and he answered, "That is Discouragement." Someone else asked, "Why is it priced higher than all these other tools when it's plain to see it is much more worn." "Because" replied the devil, "it is more useful to me than all these others. I can pry open and get into a person's head and heart with that when I cannot get near them with any other tool. Once I get inside, I can use it in whatever way suits me best. It is worn well because I use it on everyone I can, and few people ever suspect it belongs to me."

This tool was priced so high that no one could afford to buy it, and to this day it has never been sold. It still belongs to the devil, and he still uses it affectively on everyone he can. Unless we are under the blood of Jesus and a friend of the Advocate, the one seeking to sift you will devastate your life.

However, before we can call on the Advocate to be our defender, there are certain requirements. For example, there is some verses in the Bible that many Christians ignore. Proverbs 2:1-5 says,

> *My son, if you accept my words and store up my commands within you turning your ear to wisdom and applying your heart to understanding, and if you look for it as for silver and search for it as for hidden treasure, then you will understand and come to honor the Lord and find the knowledge of God.*

John 15:7-8 tells us,

> *If you remain in me and my words remain in you, ask whatever you wish, and it will be given you. This is to my Father's glory, that you bear much fruit, showing yourselves to be my followers.*

The reason God seems distant to many is found in 2 Chronicles 7:14, "If my people, who are called by my name, will humble themselves and pray and seek my face and turn from their wicked ways, then will I hear from heaven." Herein lies the rub: we will humble ourselves before God; we will pray and seek his face, but we refuse to turn from what displeases Him. "Why call me Lord, Lord," God says, "and do not the things that I say." Stop looking at the women in your office that way. I made a covenant with my eyes not to look lustfully at a girl as it says in Job 31:1. Stop the double entendre remarks and blue humour. Matthew 12:36-37 tells us that by our words we will be acquitted, and by our words we will be judged. It's a heart condition. For what's in the heart comes out of the mouth of man. And stop being coquettish and flirtatious and dressing provocatively. Stop exploiting men's weakness and vulnerability.

We will remain an entry level Christian as long as we do not take command of our flesh. We must give up in order to move up, and the higher God promotes us, the fewer options we have concerning unrestrained behavior. The spirit is willing, but the flesh is weak. This is reason enough to throw ourselves upon the Advocate.

The truth is that we cannot change on our own. We are not sinners because we sin; we sin because we are sinners. Even the great Roman philosopher, Seneca, said, "I have been seeking to climb out of the pit of my besetting sins and I cannot do it, and I never will unless a hand is let down to draw me up." We have such a one whose arm is not too short, whose hand is willing. His name is Advocate.

We are called to be holy because God is holy. God wishes, like any good parent, to break our will and conform it to His, but He does not want to break our spirit;

94

the world wants to do that. Until we allow Him to conform our will to His we have no hope of ever reaching our purpose.

Jesus said, "If anyone desires to come after me, let him deny himself." Matt. 16:24. To deny oneself is to put the interest of the Kingdom and that of others first and foremost in our life. This is not easy for we are basically self-centered, going through life saying eight words: "I want, I want, I want, I want!" What the eye admires, the heart of man desires. Jesus never promised us a rose garden. He never promised it would be easy; He only promises us a safe landing.

Because you haven't laid this book aside up to this point, here's what God could be doing in your life: He could be pouring you into a new wine skin. A quart-sized cylindrical container and a quart-sized pyramidal shaped decanter will obviously hold the same amount of liquid, but as the liquid passes from one to the other its shape changes. If the liquid had a voice, it no doubt would complain and groan as it was stretched and pulled into a new shape.

The same thing happens when God changes our shape. It is not comfortable. We have grown used to our shape. The only way we will ever live with significance and purpose is to surrender ourselves to His processes. We really must keep in mind that He is the Potter and we are the clay. We make our plans but He directs our steps. He will have His way with us, without us, or in spite of us!

In the latter stages of the of 2004 presidential election, President Bush had a line he was fond of using, "You can run but you cannot hide." God's eyes never close in sleep, and there is no darkness for God. The Bible says His eyes roam over all the earth taking in the wicked and the good. God searches the deepest motives of our hearts so that He can give to each his right reward, according to his deeds. In Jeremiah 17:9-10 it says, "Lord, you alone can heal me, you alone can save."

See to it that no one takes you captive through hollow and deceptive philosophy, Colossians 2:8-10 warns us, philosophy that depends on human tradition and the principles of this world rather than on Christ. The Advocate is Christ living in us. We have everything when we have Christ, and we are filled with God through our union with Christ. He is the highest Ruler with authority over every other power.

Careful and Prayerful

We need to be careful and prayerful. Success from God's perspective is having a good reputation, moral rectitude, character, and spiritual devotion to him. Trust and belief should be the foundation of our understanding, and we should pant after these things as a deer pants for water.

To listen is to be wise. Only a fool wants to hear the echo of his own voice. The fool is morally deficient or aggressively perverse and will eat the bitter fruit of his own stubborn ways. This is all so unnecessary.

In a society that takes overweening pride in independence and freedom, our strength tends to be our god. Our pedigree, degrees, achievements, awards, or wealth can become our walled city; God desires dependence, trust, and faith in Him alone. He does not take delight in the strength of a man or the legs of a horse.

Isaiah 1:18-20 says,

> *Come now, let us reason together; though your sins are like scarlet, they shall be as white as snow; though they are red as crimson, they shall be like wool. If you are willing and obedient (trust and obey), you will eat the best from the land.*

The real sadness with giving in to our flesh is to see how close we came to success; had we restated our belief and repeated our hope one more time, the attack might have passed and in passing given us strength for the future.

God showed that He accepted us by giving us the Holy Spirit, the Advocate. God is interested in our "want-to's"; our heartfelt desire to walk in a way pleasing in his sight. God knows our frame. When our will is weak or we are confused, remember that God's mercies never fail. When friends disappoint us or abandon us, co-workers persecute or shun us, when our own families forsake us, when we are tired of being good, we must remember that God's mercies never fail. When the dragons we fight throw us to the ground and roll over us, and God's voice seems distant, when our faults seem to hem us in and the awareness of our sins bury us in embarrassment, guilt, and shame, we must remember that God's mercies are new every morning and that they never fail. All He asks of us is that we persevere and trust in Him, have faith in Him, and believe in His Son, our Saviour, Jesus Christ.

Let me finish this chapter with a prayer I adopted from The 700 Club 24 years ago. I might alter the words from morning-to-morning so I don't simply say them by rote, but the spirit of the prayer never changes.

Dearest Lord, this day I consecrate myself to you. This day I offer myself as a living sacrifice wanting to be holy and acceptable in every way; in all of my thoughts, deeds, words, motives, attitudes and desires. And Lord, I would like for my heart to be quickened and set on fire by your Holy Spirit. Speak now to your servant in the depth of my being. Your voice which says, "This is the way walk ye in it," and this day Father, by your favor (power) I will hear and do as you say. This day, Father, I choose to obey your laws, ordinances, statutes, commandments, precepts and decrees; to believe on your testimonies in order that you might bring to full measure what is ripe in my life and what will lead me on.

Today dear precious Holy Spirit, I surrender myself to you. I yield and offer myself to you; my body with all of its working parts: my brain, my heart, my arms, hands, and fingers, my legs and feet, every fiber, every sinew, every tissue, every muscle, my bones, blood, and organs, everything!

I subordinate to you my soul with its mind, will, and emotions; all of my thoughts, passions, compulsions and appetites. I give to you all of my dreams, desires, and ambitions. Form my heart, transform my mind, and conform my will to yours Lord.

Finally, I submit to you my spirit, that indefinable and mysterious something; that breath of life that You breathed into me and only You know when I will draw my last. Blessed be Your name. Let everything that has breath praise Your name. Everything I do today I offer up as an act of worship. At the end of this day, Lord, may I know You better and love You more.

Chapter Nine

Leave Some Wiggle Room

Using Our Gifts to Serve Others

Once when comedian Charlie Chaplin was vacationing in Monaco he looked out his hotel window to see that a theatre across the street was sponsoring a Charlie Chaplin look-alike contest. Knowing that his presence in the city was unpublicized, and thinking it would be great fun, he decided to enter the contest. That evening he dressed in his baggy suit and oversized shoes, donned his funny little hat, grabbed his cane and was off to the theatre. He entered the contest and only came in third. We must know the genuine articles in life. If we are to represent God in the marketplace as His ambassadors, we must be familiar with the character traits of His Son.

A.W. Tozer said, "The reason why many are still troubled, still seeking, still making little forward progress is because they haven't yet come to the end of themselves. We're still trying to give orders, and interfering with God's work within us." If we have the truth in us, we have true riches. If we have great success, as the world knows success, we have little more than poverty.

The opening four words in Rick Warren's best selling book, *The Purpose Driven Life*, are: "It's not about you." This is directly contrary to what Madison Avenue and the world tells us. The world appeals to our predilection towards self-centeredness. There is no smaller package in the world than someone who's all wrapped up in themselves; whose world view is turned inward.

Abraham Maslow, the father of the New Age movement, devoted his entire professional life trying to prove that man is by nature good and noble rather than base and sinful. This denies the sin nature of man. To refute the folly of Maslow's premise all one has to do is observe two small children with one toy. Before long "might" will asserts itself; the older, bigger, stronger, will prevail.

To move away from this mindset we have to make a trip that moves from the head to the heart. As it took the Israelites 40 years to complete an 11-day journey, so it can take us a generation or more to complete this transition. Some never make the trip and die in their selfishness.

This all reminds me of a story about a young girl living on a farm who had a young piglet as a pet. One day she devoted many hours to scrubbing the little animal to angelic luster. But as soon she released it, it ran straight for a familiar mud hole and wallowed in it to its hearts content. After several failed attempts the little girl was beside herself with despair. Her father got an idea; he retrieved the young pig from the mud hole and took it to the town veterinarian. The vet replaced the pig's heart with a lamb's heart. From that day forward the little piglet never went near another mud hole.

God wants to form our hearts so that we have no interest in visiting the old mud holes we were once attracted to. With a new heart, our world-view will be directed outward towards others. With this new heart we will no longer lie, cheat, and steal. Our customers' and clients' best interest will be our primary concern. You can be assured that they will take notice. They may not be able to define exactly what it is they're witnessing in you, but they'll know it's real.

The payoff is something you cannot buy, trust, and people have to trust you before they'll do business with you. Believe me, you will be such a stand-out from the other salespeople that your prospects, customers, and clients deal with that you will find your business on the increase.

The bigger payoff will come in the form of the fruits of the Spirit, which all emanate from true love. They are: joy, peace, patience, kindness, goodness, faithfulness, gentleness, and self-control. You'll have a peace that transcends all understanding. In a world where people live in a perpetual state of fear and frustration, anxiety and confusion, you will have calm. This is, in itself, a strong testimony. People will want to know what it is you have that the world cannot give them.

The opposite or misuse of love is: jealousy, anger, impatience, frustration, rudeness, selfishness, guile, hot headedness, pride, gossip, and carrying grudges. This kind of emotional and psychological existence will consume you from the inside out.

Living, really living, results in victory and not merely deliverance.

An old saying goes, "If God is your Father, act worthy of the family name." Once you know that you are in Christ, you will realize that you are unique; there has never been, nor will there ever be, another human being exactly like you. This is tremendously liberating because it gives us freedom to be who we were created to be. This obliterates feelings of inferiority. You are perfectly made to accomplish what God designed you to be and do.

We are all familiar with the saying, "The truth will set you free!" This means being free from trying to impress others or ceaselessly emulating them. We are born unique; unfortunately, most of us die copies. We will be free from the "fear of man." We should respect all men but deify and fear no one. It means freedom from making promises we cannot keep. It means freedom from moral relativism that says morality is based on circumstances; that if no one gets hurt, that if no one sees me, or if I don't get caught, then I haven't technically done anything wrong. Freedom means deliverance from buying things we don't need or can't afford to impress people we don't like.

Selling is about filling a need. Marketing is revealing a need people don't know they have. Companies employ marketing geniuses and spend millions of dollars in advertising to create or appeal to what is referred to as the "itch factor." With a mind-set that says, "You've got our money in your pocket, and our objective is to get our money out of your pocket and into our bank account," they try to convince you that you need their product or service in order to be among the "in" crowd; to be acceptable. As they are well aware, being accepted is one of the greatest cries of the human heart. We buy things to be "cool." We buy things to make us feel better or elevate a sagging self image. The insecure place their self-worth in what they own, what they can do, or who they know. When I'm asked to autograph one of my books at a conference or seminar, I frequently ask the person for their autograph just to remind them that we are equals; God is no respecter of persons.

We all need to make a living and that's legitimate, but we need to keep in mind Deuteronomy 8:18-19,

> It is the Lord your God who gives you the ability to produce wealth. And it shall come about if you ever forget the Lord your God, and go after other gods and serve them and worship them, I testify against you today that you shall surely perish.

I find it difficult to believe that God is pleased when we "load people up" with goods or services they do not need. This is loving money and using people. To say, "They should know better; if they can't afford it they shouldn't buy it" is not righteous. It doesn't square with being my brother's keeper. There is no softer pillow than a clear conscience. If my conscience is so seared that I don't give pause to reflect upon my actions of the day, I am stuck in deep mud.

A young man working for a bank was once being considered for promotion to vice-president. The president of the bank met with his senior vice-presidents to discuss the merits of the promotion. One of the senior vice-presidents said he could not vote in favor of the young man because he had observed him in the cafeteria the day before slipping something under the lip of his plate in order to avoid having to pay for it. He realized that if a person would steal a piece of straw, he would steal a camel. Stealing is stealing. Stealing, cheating, lying cuts us off from God's favor. Another word for favor is grace, and grace is the ability to accomplish, to do.

Everything grows. This is why those harmless "white lies" are like the little foxes that steal the grapes. Lying to customers about shipping dates in order to beat the competition spawns more lying. To withhold payment, commissions, or a promotion from those deserving, is lying. Lying on your expense account, putting the "disabled" sign in your car window to get a favored parking position, is lying and cheating. Then we wonder why God does not bless our efforts. If God cannot trust us with a short leash, He will never entrust us with a long one. He knows that we'll get entangled in it. To find ourselves strangers to favor insures a lean and unproductive life. The empty headed or morally adrift treat life as a plaything; it's all a big game or contest to them. The truth of the matter is that as God's representatives we are supposed to be bringing order to chaos. We are in training for reigning. Putting off immediate gratification for long term gains is one definition of maturity.
Salespeople are especially adept at lying to themselves. They are highly skilled at rationalizing or making up alibis. I had a salesperson explain it this way: There's

nothing going on in January because everyone's recovering from Christmas in January. February all the good buyers and customers have gone to warmer climates for the winter. In March you can't talk to anyone because they're too busy preparing their income taxes. April is the Easter season, and besides, you know how unpredictable and stormy the weather can be in April. May is the first nice month and so all the prospects are out on the golf course. In June everyone's preoccupied with graduations. In July everyone's on vacation. And in August everyone's still on vacation. In September everybody's getting their kids back in school. In October everyone's waiting to see how inventories will come out. In November everybody's too upset over the elections. And in December Christmas is coming, and besides, you know nobody writes any business in December. This salesman had only about seven days a year in which to do any business. He was the kind of salesperson who orders 500 business cards in January, and the following December still has 480 cards left. We are past masters at making excuses to ourselves.

What's your standard? We all have a standard by which we conduct ourselves. Is it Wall Street? Is it a rapacious company who cares little for their customers? Is it the gospel of self? Is your standard based on your feelings? As Napoleon Bonaparte lay dying at the age of 51 said,

I die before my time and my body shall be given

back to the earth and devoured by worms. What an abysmal gulf between my deep miseries and the eternal Kingdom of Christ. I marvel that whereas the ambitious dreams of myself and of Alexander and of Caesar should have vanished into thin air, a Judean peasant — Jesus — should be able to stretch his hands across the centuries, and control the destinies of men and nations.

Like the Marines, God is looking for a few good men (people). "Most of the shadows of fear and doubt," Emerson said, "are caused by man standing in his own sunlight." We get in our own way. We get in God's way. We think we know best, or how to take a short-cut. Regardless of how many college degrees we accumulate, knowledge never leads to wisdom. Knowledge only leads to more knowledge. Wisdom includes knowing truth, but primarily it has to do with a skill in how to live. This is why I can say declaratively that it is impossible to lead a meaningful life, a life of character and virtue if we do not know the Author of life. Some well meaning and even long-standing Christians have a faith that is a mile wide but only inches deep. Better to be narrow and deep than wide and shallow. Will we be one of those few good people God is looking for?

If so, we must come to a place where we acknowledge and accept that God is large and in charge, and we need to resign from our steering committee. Someone once said that God leads through circumstances; Jesus leads through his word, the Bible; and the Holy Spirit leads through the still quiet voice known as our conscience. We need to get into God's Word.

Sigmund Freud took away our guilt but gave us anxiety. Understanding God gives us direction, balance, and peace. Where life can sometimes cause despair, God gives us hope. Where society says "You can't do it, you're too young or too old, or you're not smart enough," God says, "All things are possible to them that believe." One word thunders throughout all of Scripture: TRIUMPH! TRIUMPH! TRIUMPH! When someone is being run over by life, I like to ask them three questions: Are you praying? Are you getting to know the Author of life through the gift of His Word? A gift unopened is useless. Are you associating with like minded people; who are you hanging around with? When life knocks you to your knees, that's a pretty good position in which to pray.

Do you rule over your problems or do your problems rule over you? Jesus said, "I come so that you might have life and have it abundantly" (John 10:10). All believers have life but not all believers have abundant life. Abundant life is God's norm. Many Christians today are living a "religion of form" but no power. I have been broke financially several times is my life, but I've never been poor. Even in my wild years and mad existence, I knew that God was my Father and had better things for me. Eventually I realized that doubts result from a lack of resolution and that produces a withering slow growth paralysis. A house divided against itself cannot long stand.

If you enjoy sales, unquestionably you are looking for success. But what is success? Proverbs 22:4 defines success as favor. Favor is the key to success. The one who finds favor from God receives riches, honor, and life. The world refers to these things as, wealth or money, recognition or prestige, and health.

The world does not have a clue as to how to attain these things in a meaningful way. Most Christians are even at a loss about how to achieve these things. Riches, honor, and life are rewards of humility. Humility means serving, and this is not a popular concept in 21st century thinking. Most of us want to be served; we're not too interested in serving. Yet this is another of the Kingdom's great principles of success. "But he that is greatest among you," Jesus said, "will be your servant." We are either into titles or we are into towels. Whoever humbles himself shall be exalted.

A true servant's heart requires humility and meekness. It is said that Moses was the most humble man who ever lived. Yet Moses killed a man during a fight, so we know he was no shrinking violet. When we hear the word "meek" today, we think of some milquetoast obsequious little bootlicker who's never had a strong opinion in his life. But actually the word meek is taken from the Greek word *pross*. Pross was a war-horse in ancient Greece and it took great skill and was considered a high honor to train one of these horses. The horse could not panic in battle. It had to be taught to respond to leg and heel pressure for the rider's hands would be engaged with sword and shield.

To insure that all will end well in our endeavors, we need to listen to Jesus' words from the Sermon on the Mount, for the Kingdom of God still rules in the affairs of men. In Matthew 6:31-33 Jesus says, "But seek first the Kingdom of God and His righteousness, and all these things will be added unto you."

Answer to puzzle:

About the Author

Published author, columnist, and humorist, John Grogan, has spoken in every major city in America, Canada, England, Australia, and New Zealand. In fact, this laugh merchant has traveled in excess of 100,000 miles – just on airport moving walkways! For more than three decades he has delighted business groups, sales congresses, churches, and association conventions, with his Irish wit and certifiably funny stories.

After college and serving in the military, John completed an aptitude test showing that his best chances for advancement lie with a firm closely supervised by his father.? After joining his father's real estate firm he spent several years in the field selling, and then became a manager. With his emphasis on working effectively with people, and finding significance and purpose in work and in life, he led his office to top honors. At the invitation of American Motivational Association, he spoke to business and sales groups all across North America. He then went on to work as a training instructor for Dun & Bradstreet.

Dr. Norman Vincent Peale, after being on a program with John, said "I have never heard so much useful information dispensed in such a short period of time."

A long time leader in his church, The Grace Place, John is a past member of the Board of Trustees. He currently is a greeter and usher, and serves on the Ministry Vision & Leadership Team coordinating evangelism outreach. He has been selected to be the point man for the highly acclaimed Celebrate Recovery program.

John has written three books published by the Christian publishing house, Evergreen Press. His latest book, *Help, I've Fallen & Need A Good Laugh!* is the basis for his live performance of Living With Passion, Purpose, Power & Laughter!

John is a cancer survivor and lives outside of Nashville, Tennessee with Jackie, his wife of twenty-two years.

John Grogan
49 Chandler-Radford Rd.
Mt. Juliet, TN 37122
Call: 615.758.9713 /
Toll Free: 877.904. HELP(4357)
Fax: 615.758.6770
E-mail: johngrogan@skyquest.net
Website under re-construction

Other books by John Grogan

PROVERBS OF SUCCESS
Learn how to excel at being of service to others.
ISBN 1-58169-045-2   96 pg.   PB $5.99

GOLD NUGGETS AND SILVER BULLETS
Stories and insights that impart new wisdom for your life and career.
ISBN 1-58169-113-0   128 pg.   PB $9.99

HELP I'VE FALLEN AND NEED A GOOD LAUGH
When life slams you to the floor, you need a pick-me-up. Grogan's stories will get you laughing and help put things into perspective. Includes more than 100 humorous stories.
ISBN 1-58169-160-2   128 pg.   PB $9.99